Aginc

Gordon Corrigan

Copyright © Gordon Corrigan 2024.

The right of Gordon Corrigan to be identified as the author of this work has been asserted by him in accordance with the Copyright, Designs and Patents Act, 1988.

First published in 2024 by Sharpe Books.

AGINCOURT

Introduction

The Hundred Years War was the longest war in England's military history. It was by no means a period of continual fighting, being punctuated by treaties and periods of peace, but as English aims remained consistent from 1337 to 1453, actually 116 years, through the reigns of five English kings and six French ones, it is reasonable to consider it as one war. The ostensible cause was the English claim to the throne of France as of right. Phillip IV of France died in 1314 and his three sons ruled after him in turn, none producing a legitimate heir. When the last son, and the last of the Capetian kings, Charles IV died in 1328 his nearest male relative was King Edward III of England, first cousin of Charles IV and grandson of Phillip IV through his mother, Phillip's daughter. The French were not prepared to allow the French throne to be occupied by a scion of the traditional enemy, England, and instead gave it to Phillip of Anjou who was only a nephew of Philip IV. Then there was the longstanding question of Aquitaine, English since 1152 when Henry II of England married Eleanor of Aquitaine. Was it held by the king of England in full sovereignty, as England claimed, or did he hold it as a vassal of the king of France, as the latter alleged? Along with these English objectives was the more practical wish to recover English lands in France lost by King John in the thirteenth century. This book is the fourth, and last, in a series based on the major battles of the war. Although each book stands alone, they cover the battles of Sluys 1340, Crecy 1346, Poitiers 1356 and Agincourt 1415. There were of course many other battles, combats and skirmishes, many also covered in the four books, and the claim to the French throne was not formally abandoned until the negotiations for the Peace of Amiens in 1801, during yet another prolonged period of warfare against Revolutionary and then Napoleonic France.

Chapter One – After Poitiers

Despite the great victory of Poitiers in 1356 the latter years of the Fourteenth Century did not advance England's cause in the Hundred Years War. In a strange way the victory hindered any chance of an acceptance of England's demands and an end of the war, for those in France who could have arrived at that happy conclusion were dead or, like the French king, a prisoner in the Tower of London with his ransom as yet unpaid. English ambitions were further hampered by the death of the Black Prince in 1376 and of his father the following year. While King Edward had become increasingly conservative and in thrall to a greedy mistress, he was nevertheless one of our greatest kings who had unified the country from the in-fighting and instability of his father's reign and the subsequent unwelcome influence of Mortimer. The Black Prince may not have been an entirely successful administrator, and he had caused unrest in Aquitaine due to his taxation policies, but he was a military commander without equal and was of a sufficiently robust and intelligent character to have been a great king.

With the death of both the king and his heir apparent, the throne now passed to Richard II, the ten-year-old child of the Black Prince and Joan of Kent. That union was unusual, for royal marriages were normally made for purely dynastic purposes – to cement an alliance, to neutralise an opponent or to gain the support of a powerful family. The Black Prince's marriage at the age of thirty-one to Joan, aged thirty-three, brought no political advantage. She was the daughter of the Earl of Kent and a granddaughter of King Edward I and in 1340 at the age of twelve she secretly married Thomas Holland, a twenty-six-year-old gentleman, the younger son of a knight but landless and far below her in station. At that time the church permitted sexual intercourse at the age of twelve for girls provide they had passed puberty. Joan had failed to obtain royal permission for the marriage, as was required for relatives of the royal family, but the marriage was nonetheless legal and was consummated.

AGINCOURT

Shortly after the marriage Holland went off campaigning in Prussia with the Teutonic Knights and while he was away Joan's mother arranged for her to be married to William Montagu, heir to the Earl of Salisbury, a much more advantageous match than that with Holland. Joan said later that she had not told her mother of the marriage with Holland as she feared he might be arrested and charged with treason. From then on Holland rose up the military ranks. He went to Flanders in the first military expedition of King Edward III and fought at Sluys. Later he fought at Crecy and had proved his military ability, acquired considerable riches from ransomed prisoners and been knighted, being one of the founder members of the Order of the Garter. On return from the Crecy expedition in 1347 he felt sufficiently confident to begin legal procedures to demand the return of his wife and in 1349 a papal bull declared his original marriage lawful and ordered the return of Joan.

Holland and Joan had five children between them, four of whom reached adulthood. Sir Thomas held a number of important independent commands and eventually was sent to Normandy as the King's lieutenant to enforce the provisions of the Treaty of Brétigny. That treaty was the consequence of the victory of Poitiers, and while it had been agreed and signed by the French king Jean, a prisoner in England, it was repudiated by the dauphin and the government in Paris. In 1360, at the age of forty-six, Sir Thomas Holland died suddenly in Rouen, probably of dysentery, a not uncommon affliction at the time. The following year the Black Prince sought Joan's hand in marriage. They had known each other as children, he was thirty-one, she thirty-three. Contrary to all the accepted rules in regard to royal marriages, this sems to have been a genuine love match. They had two children, Edward who died aged seven, and Richard, who would succeed his grandfather in 1377. Four years after the Black Prince's marriage the French king, Jean II died in London. We do not know the cause of his death – he had been well treated in captivity – but it may have been the last flicker of the plague, which had reappeared in 1361, although with far less severity than in 1348. Jean's son was now proclaimed as king of France.

When an English king has been incompetent, incapable or a child English ambitions turn inwards, and so it was with Richard, as magnates jockeyed for control, position and influence. In his early years the government of England was carried out in the king's name by a succession of regency councils, although as Richard grew older he had more and more influence on their decisions. The efforts of those wishing a permanent peace in the war, which Richard almost certainly did, suffered a setback when the French Pope Gregory XI died in 1378 and the conclave of cardinals elected an Italian, Bartolomeo Prignano, as Urban VI. The French refused to accept his election and put forward their own candidate, Cardinal Robert of Geneva, who although Swiss by birth had spent most of his time in France, and acclaimed him as Pope Clement VII. Thus began the Great Western Schism, with Urban in Rome recognised by England and Clement in Avignon supported by France and Scotland. Previously, while the popes were regarded with great suspicion by the English, they did at least provide a forum for peace negotiations. Now with the schism that option was gone and there was no professedly disinterested single body to act as a go between.

For all his faults as a king – and they were many – no one could doubt Richard's courage as he faced what is known as the Peasants' Revolts of 1381, the same year that Jean II of France died. Although many of those who rebelled against the system were indeed peasants, the name is a misnomer for there were many of the gentry and merchant classes who were actively involved, as were disgruntled minor officials and demobilised soldiers. The causes were many but they stretched back to the great plague of 1348, the Black Death, which killed off perhaps fifty percent of the population. This meant that the same amount of land had only half the available labour force to till it, and so with a labour shortage labourers could now demand higher wages and move around the country seeking the best deal. This rapid increase in wages caused inflation and led to Edward III enacting the Ordinance of Labourers in 1349 and following it with the Statute of Labourers in 1351. This act ordered that rates of pay were to revert to those in force before the plague, specifically to those of

AGINCOURT

1346, and forbade labourers from moving from their established place of residence. Additionally it said than all men who were physically capable were required to have a job – there were to be no unemployed. At the time, with a popular king, success in the war, incomes of the landowners increased by ransom payments and loot from France, much of which trickled down, there was some grumbling but no threat to the established order. In any case the enforcement of the act was cursory at best. Later, after the death of the Black Prince and his father and stalemate in the war, with less gold and spoils coming into the country, it was a major factor in the eventual revolt.

On the accession of the ten year old king the government was placed in the hands of a regency council of fourteen members, which included the archbishop of Canterbury, several bishops, and the powerful magnates of the day, but significantly excluded John of Gaunt, son of Edward III and the king's uncle, who was generally suspected (probably wrongly) of ambitions towards the kingship himself. Generally taxation to pay for the ongoing war came from custom duties and a levy on 'moveable property' and on the church, which did not directly impinge on the peasantry or the labouring classes, but in 1377, on the accession of Richard, the regency council declared a poll tax. This was a tax of one groat (4d, 2.7p or worth around £15 today), now to be levied on every individual over the age of fourteen, except for beggars, regardless of means and was highly unpopular with widespread evasion. The poll tax was levied again in 1379, with the age limit raised to sixteen this time, and again in 1381. The 1381 levy ought to have been fairer for although the age limit was reduced to fifteen, this time it was graded. Everyone paid the basic one groat but those able to afford it paid more, with those responsible for gathering the tax being required to account for an average of three groats, or one shilling, per head of the population for which they were responsible. This had unfortunate consequences, as collectors coerced populations, particularly in rural areas where the peasantry were less educated, to get more than the average so that they could pocket whatever was in excess of the one shilling per head demanded by central government.

While social mobility in the army was well established – men who proved themselves on the battlefield could expect advancement – this was not the case generally, and radical itinerant preachers such as John Ball, aged forty-three in 1381, were travelling around the country, in Ball's case chiefly in Kent, attacking the existing social order of King – Nobility – Gentry and Others. He claimed that God created all men as equal (to Ball is attributed 'When Adam delved and Eve span, who was then the Gentleman?') and while Ball's rhetoric was attractive to the 'have nots' it was anathema to those responsible for upholding the existing social order, including the church, and Ball, though a priest, was imprisoned several times.

While all the above factors contributed to the rebellion, it was really a mass protest against misgovernment of those around the King. It started in Kent in May 1381 where a group of villagers and tenant farmers refused to pay the poll tax, scragged the tax collectors and hounded them out. Rioting spread throughout Kent and Essex, where a senior judge, sent to investigate, was set upon. Realising that they had crossed a line and that retribution would follow, the delinquents decided to pre-empt whatever was coming and march on London. Gathering in Canterbury and egged on by Ball and his like the mob grew, enhanced by those who had a grievance, those who saw an opportunity for genuine reform and the usual hangers-on who went along for the fun and the plunder. As usual, it was not the King who was the object of their discontent but his advisers, and the cry was taken up 'King Richard and the true Commons'. The leader, or at least the ostensible leader for there must have been men of education and military experience to advise him, was Wat Tyler. Not much is known about him, he is thought to have been about forty years old, his first name may have been the old English name of Watt, or a shortening of Walter, and his second name may have simply referred to his occupation of putting tiles on roofs.

Armed with a variety of weapons the rebels advanced on London, opening prisons and burning court records as they went. As they got nearer the King, the royal family, the Chancellor (the archbishop of Canterbury) and most of the regency council took

AGINCOURT

refuge in the Tower of London, among them Henry Bolingbroke, son of John of Gaunt and a cousin of the King of the same age. The rebels found the drawbridge of London Bridge, the only crossing of the Thames at that time, was up and thus barred their way into the city. Moving south along the river they sacked the archbishop's palace at Lambeth, opened Southwark prison and sent a message to the Tower asking to speak to the King. The King agreed and on 13 June he was rowed four miles down the river by royal barge to Rotherhithe, where a large crowd of rebels were massed on the bank. Richard's advisers considered it was too dangerous for him to land so he spoke to them from the barge, asking what they wanted. The spokesman for the rebels, probably not Wat Tyler at this stage, said that they wanted the heads of the Chancellor, the Chief Justice and the Treasurer, and the dismissal of evil counsellors. The King gave the diplomatic reply that, within the law, they could have whatever heads they wanted, and was rowed back to the Tower.

Shortly after this, contrary to the express orders of the Lord Mayor of London, Sir William Walworth, that on no account was the London Bridge drawbridge to be lowered, a sympathiser did lower it and the rebels were into the city. They looted John of Gaunt's Savoy palace (where the Savoy hotel is now), released the occupants of the Fleet and Newgate prisons and, almost inevitably, slaughtered any foreigners they could find, mostly Flemings and Jews. The King agreed to meet them again, at Mile End, in the East End, on 14 June. There the demands were repeated, but now, in addition to the heads of those they disliked, were added political reforms: the abolition of serfdom and villeinage (bonded and indentured labour), equality for all below the king (the nobility to be abolished), a fixed rent of four pence an acre for land[*] and an amnesty for all involved in the rising. The King said he would grant all the demands and rode back to the Tower. Arriving there he found that a group of rebels had forced an entry and had dragged out the Chancellor, Archbishop Sudbury, and the

---

[*] About £15 at today's values. Currently agricultural land in Kent can be rented for between £72 and £34 per acre.

Treasurer, Sir Robert Hales, and had beheaded them both on Tower Hill. Henry Bolingbroke was lucky to avoid a similar fate.

The steam now was out of the rebellion, and assuming all their demands had been achieved, most now dispersed and began to return home, except for group of diehards under Wat Tyler, who presumably wanted further assurances and asked to meet the King again. It was agreed that the King would meet them on Sunday 15 June at Smithfield. That morning the King left the Tower with the Lord Mayor of London and an escort of around 200 mounted men-at-arms. On arrival at Smithfield the King's party arrayed themselves at one end of the field, with the rebels at the other. Wat Tyler was invited to come and talk to the King and he rode across to the royal party. What happened next is related in numerous contemporary accounts all of which differ! All do however agree that the Lord Mayor stabbed Tyler, who fell to the ground. Whether this was in reaction to an aggressive move by Tyler towards the King, or a misunderstanding, or whether it was always the intention to arrest Tyler is not known. Whatever the reason for the stabbing, seeing their leader fall to the ground a number of ex archers among the rebels unslung their bows and began to nock arrows. Showing considerable courage for a fourteen-year-old, or perhaps as a spoilt child he had no conception of danger, the King cantered across the field to the rebel ranks. Drawing his sword he announced that the men should consider him, the King, as their leader and that he would lead them to Clerkenwell where they would be fed and he would confirm the granting of all their demands. At this stage someone, possibly the Lord Mayor, galloped off into the city to raise soldiers and armed civilians to concentrate at Clerkenwell. When the rebels reached there they were either surrounded and dispersed by force or persuaded to leave the city and return to their homes peaceably, while the dying Tyler was rushed to Tyburn and hanged.

With the dispersal of the mob from London the rebellion petered out, and all was left was for the authorities to mop up. As at this stage the council considered that reconciliation was preferable to revenge, only a very few of the most egregious participants were put on trial. As there were complicated legal arguments as to what exactly constituted treason, most were charged with varying degrees of felony. One exception was John Ball, who was put on trial in Coventry charged with treason, allowed to speak in his own defence, found guilty and sentenced to a traitor's death. On 15 July he was drawn, hung and quartered in St Albans with his head put on a spike on London Bridge and his four quarters despatched to four other towns. Other than that, repercussions were relatively mild, but when shortly afterwards another flare up occurred in Essex there was no mercy, with all those involved executed or imprisoned. Needless to say the King did not keep any of his promises, the argument being that promises extracted under duress had no validity. For the next seven years the government of the country was in the hands of councils of varying composition, and the war descended into minor skirmishes on land and coastal raids by sea.

In France the government and the administration had effectively broken down. The treasury was empty, fields were untilled, starvation was rife and most of the peasantry just wanted peace at any price. There were risings against excessive taxation, savagely put down, and while those nobles who had not been killed or taken prisoner at Poitiers wanted the war to continue, there was little money to pay for it. The new king, Charles V, known to the French chroniclers as *Carolus Sapiens* in tribute to his library of over 1,000 books in the Louvre, was sickly, of insignificant appearance and no soldier, but he was no fool either. He had no intention of accepting the new status of the English in France, but was too much of a lawyer to attempt to oppose it openly, rather he would whittle away at English possessions and try to undermine their government rather than attempt to confront them militarily, which he was experienced enough to know he could not do – at least not yet. He was a far greater threat to the English than either of his Valois predecessors. The problems facing Charles were reduced when Duke John of Brittany, put in place by the English, accepted that he held that duchy as a fief of the king of France (as in law he did) and paid homage to Charles for it. In Brittany at least there would be relative stability.

What Charles had to do was to try to limit the depredations of the *routiers*. These were independent companies, more often the size of brigades, of mercenaries, consisting of many demobilised soldiers, mainly Gascons but with Flemings, Germans, Italians and Spanish too, mostly led by Englishmen who had done well out of the war and wanted to continue to enrich themselves now that major battles with the opportunities of ransom were no longer available. The routier companies had strict rules as to the division of spoils, a proper chain of command and in most cases a uniform. They had become accustomed to life as soldiers and to being able to burn and plunder as they liked, and saw no reason to stop doing so just because there was now peace between England and France. Nearly all mounted they moved the length and breadth of French occupied France, Italy and Spain looting and burning and holding hostage anybody who looked like being rich enough to pay for their release. Leaders included Sir John Hawkwood, the son of a tanner and minor landowner, Sir Robert Knollys, of Cheshire yeoman stock, both having started their military careers as archers, and Sir Hugh Calveley, younger son of a knight with little land. These men, and others like them, had made their names in Edward III's wars, had risen up the ranks and been knighted and were typical of the social mobility provided by service in the army. King Edward was happy to ignore their depredations provided they did not claim to act in his name, and even Richard made little attempt to rein them in, only occasionally issuing a warrant, rarely executed, for breaching the terms of any Anglo-French treaty that might be in force.

In England relations between the King and his counsellors, including his uncle the Duke of Gloucester, were often strained, and on one occasion the council asked that the Chancellor, Richard de la Pole, Earl of Suffolk, be dismissed because they considered his foreign policy to be disastrous because it failed to capitalise on the gains of Poitiers and had allowed John of Brittany to shift his allegiance. Richard replied that he would not dismiss a scullion from his kitchen on their say so, and that if his subjects opposed him he would seek help from his cousin, the king of France. This was going too far and when Gloucester reminded him that kings

AGINCOURT

had been deposed in the past, reminding him of the fate of his own grandfather, Edward II, Richard backed off and dismissed Suffolk. Increasingly Richard found himself at odds with the great men of the kingdom. He felt that with the treasury bare, Scottish border raids increasing and the greatly increased cost of shipments from Bordeaux, which now had to be escorted, he wanted an end to the war. This might have been a sensible course but it was not acceptable to those who wanted to hold on to lands in France, nor to the common soldiery whose only hope of riches and advancement lay in a continuance of the war. These conflicting views brought the country to the brink of civil war, with the King personally hiring and paying soldiers who wore his personal badge, a white hart, rather than the accepted badge for English armies of the cross of St George. The Lords Appellant, as those opposed to the King called themselves, had their way in 1388 when the so called merciless parliament sentenced five of the King's favourites to death as traitors. For the moment the king had no choice but to accept it, but he would have his revenge in due course.

In 1389 Richard declared that henceforth he would reign without benefit of council, and as he was twenty-two years old he was perfectly entitled to do so, unwise though it may have been. The same year he negotiated a temporary truce, to last until something more permanent could be arranged. As it involved the English giving up the ports of Brest and Cherbourg this brought mutterings from the Lord Appellant but as yet no action, and this peace did last for the next few years. Richard had married his first wife, Anne of Bohemia, in 1382 when he was fifteen and she a year older, but she died of plague in 1394. Although they had no children, Anne was, to some, extent, a moderating influence on Richard and his behaviour certainly deteriorated after her death. In 1396 he married again, this time to Isobel the nine years old daughter of Charles VI of France[*].

---

[*] He had succeeded his father Charles V in 1380. For much of his reign government was in the hands of a regency, as he was prone to frequent bouts of madness.

GORDON CORRIGAN

The marriage ceremony was held in English Calais where Richard made a statement that he can have had no idea of its repugnance to all levels of English society (or if he did know he clearly did not care). He promised that he would work with the French to depose Pope Urban and have Pope Clement at Avignon recognised as the only legitimate heir to the keys of Saint Peter. In England there was outrage, not only amongst the clergy who saw themselves abandoned by their king, but by the laity who saw it as playing into French hands. Richard cared not a jot. His dowry from the French on marriage was £170,000[*], enough for him to recruit even more soldiers and take the next step to avenge the deaths of his friends nine years previously. In July 1397 he ordered the arrest of Gloucester, Arundel and Warwick, the senior members of the Lords Appellant. Gloucester was conveyed to Calais and quietly murdered, probably by smothering: he was, after all, the son of a king, while Arundel, Warwick and their adherents were tried before Richard's equivalent of the merciless parliament, with John of Gaunt presiding. In September Arundel was sentenced to death and executed, while Warwick was awarded life imprisonment. Henry Bolingbroke, Gaunt's son, had at one stage joined the Lords Appellant but although he had been pardoned on the grounds that he had moderated their demands, he was now seen as a potential threat and exiled, banished for ten years.

As Richard's rule descended into a tyranny of forced loans, increasing disregard for the laws and customs of the realm, an insistence that the king ruled by God's choice and not that of the people, more and more luxury at court and his adoption of the title 'majesty' – the first time this had been used by an English king – opposition grew. John of Gaunt had raised no objection to the fate of his brother Gloucester, nor to the exile of his son, at least not publicly, and as far as we can tell he remained a loyal supporter of the crown to the end, although what he might have told his son and how he may have advised him can only be supposition. In 1398 Richard at last got what he wanted and needed in his foreign relations, when a twenty-eight-year truce was agreed with France.

---

[*] About £12 million today.

AGINCOURT

John of Gaunt died in 1399 and Richard then finally went too far: he extended Henry Bolingbroke's banishment from ten years to life and confiscated the duchy of Lancaster with all its castles, lands and titles. This was the final straw for the magnates, for if the king could do this to the duchy of Lancaster, whose lands might be next? Unaware, or uncaring, of the reaction in the country to his arbitrary actions, Richard set off for Ireland where that unhappy country was once more in a state of unrest, and Henry Bolingbroke saw his chance. Henry had spent much of his exile in Paris, and elements of the French nobility were more than ready to help and support him. Henry, with only about fifty personal retainers, fellow exiles and men-at-arms took ship at Boulogne sometime in June 1399, having given out the cover story that he was off on a pilgrimage to the Holy Land, and landed somewhere in the Humber estuary at the end of the month. As he moved through Yorkshire knights and magnates declared their support for him and joined him with their retinues. At this stage Henry does not seem to have had any intention of deposing Richard: only of regaining his Lancastrian heritage and removing Richard's 'evil counsellors'. Once the earl of Northumberland and his son, Henry Percy ('Hotspur') came over to him Henry was assured of the support of the north, and with the defection of Edmund Duke of York, the king's uncle and regent during Richard's absence in Ireland and the submission of the Ricardian stronghold of Chester without a fight, Richard's spies knew that the situation was serious. In Ireland Richard was indecisive and even when ships were found to embark his army he changed his mind as to the port of departure and unloading and then loading men and horses wasted more time. Eventually the king landed in Wales and his soldiers began slipping away. With a few trusted advisers he took refuge in Conway Castle.

When the earl of Northumberland arrived as Henry's emissary the king was persuaded to give himself up and was taken to London and lodged in the Tower. At some stage, probably when the Duke of York had gone over to him, Henry elected to aim for the throne itself, rather than just regaining what he considered to be his rightful due. Knowing how duplicitous Richard could be, he presumably decided that he could not risk leaving Richard on the throne plotting revenge, but the question was how to assume the crown in a manner that could be portrayed as legal. The deposition of Edward II was not a true precedent as he had been replaced by the next in line, his son Edward III, whereas Richard's immediate heir was not Henry but another cousin, the eight year old Edmund Mortimer, third Earl of March, whose mother Philippa was a daughter of Lionel of Antwerp, Edward III's second son, whereas Henry was the son of the third son. As the English claim to the French throne was based on inheritance through the female line, Edmund's claim could not be dismissed on those grounds, and the justices strongly advised against claiming the throne by right of conquest, as being the wrong message to send to other potential usurpers. Eventually, on 29 September 1399, Richard's twenty-two-year reign came to an end when he was persuaded to relinquish the crown to Henry, although there was much legal fudge to justify it. Quite how Richard was 'persuaded' to agree, or whether in fact he did agree, we do not know but Henry was acclaimed by Parliament and duly crowned on 13 October. He would reign as Henry IV and Richard was despatched to the Lancastrian stronghold of Pontefract.

Sometime in December a conspiracy to restore Richard was discovered. Of the chief plotters Salisbury was lynched by a mob in Gloucester, Despenser murdered in Bristol and Huntingdon caught and beheaded in Essex. As long as Richard lived he was bound to be the focus for those who opposed the new regime, and like Edward II before him his demise would be convenient, and the sooner the better. Only one chronicle suggests that Richard was murdered, by being hacked into pieces, others variously claim that he was starved to death by his jailers, that he deliberately starved himself or that he died of grief. The body was removed from Pontefract to London, and as there were regular stops on the way so that the body could be exhibited to the public, the hacked into pieces theory can be discounted. Nobody actually dies of

AGINCOURT

grief, and as death by starvation, whether forced or self-inflicted*, can take an inconveniently long time, we may reasonably suppose that Richard II was done to death in the usual way when the body of a high born personage must be exhibited – by suffocation – and as it was in his interests that Richard should die, that Henry IV ordered it.

---

* In 1981 the imprisoned IRA terrorist 'Bobby' Sands went on hunger strike in the mistaken belief that the British government would not wish him to die and would concede the prisoners' demands. The government held no such view and while the smart money was on a period of thirty days, Sands lasted for sixty-six days before dying. As an indication of the level of intelligence of that organisation, another nine hunger strikers followed Sands to the grave before the IRA realised that the British would not give in.

Chapter Two: The first Lancastrian

As a young man Henry Bolingbroke exhibited all the qualities of kingship that his cousin, the rightful king, did not have. A champion jouster and an experienced soldier, his usurpation of the throne was generally welcomed by the population and most of the great magnates supported his accession. He should have been a popular and effective king. The problem of a disputed or not entirely legal succession, however, is that it leaves the way open for objectors to the regime to claim that it is illegitimate and cannot therefore levy taxes, wage war, make land grants, treat with foreign powers or exercise any of the other myriad tasks faced by a royal government. Throughout his nine year reign Henry was plagued by a shortage of money, unruly magnates, the Scots, the French the Welsh and, finally, an uncooperative son.

It had not, however, escaped the notice of Henry's subjects that he had inherited not only the vast wealth of the Duchy of Lancaster but also that of his wife, Mary Bohun, co-heiress to the earl of Hereford. Mary gave Henry four sons (the eldest the future Henry V) and two daughters before dying giving birth to Philippa in 1394, with her wealth passing to Henry. All that added to the income of the crown should, it was not unreasonably supposed, have been more than sufficient to fund the court and run the country, but Henry had made large grants of land and money to buy the loyalty of Richard II's adherents and to reward his own followers, had rather unwisely given the impression that he did not intend to tax harshly (which many took to mean not at all), and as he had little or no experience of government was not able administratively to control court expenditure. While parliament did grant him the customs duties on wool, exports of wool were down significantly and so was money from that source. Throughout his reign Henry was unable to live within his means, and as one of his rallying cries was repudiation of the peace-making policy of Richard, then a resumption of the war was going to mean a requirement for even more money.

AGINCOURT

In France the removal of Richard and his replacement by Henry was regarded with horror. While claiming to object to the deposing of a rightful king, the real French objection was that Henry might resume the war and reject the truce agreed by Richard. France in any case was in turmoil. In 1392 Charles VI, the Valois king, had gone barking (literally) mad, the first manifestation being his setting on and slaying members of his entourage, developing into wandering around the palace howling like a dog, and a conviction that he was made of glass. While casual killing and the occasional bark might not matter overmuch, a belief that one is made of glass rather militates against taking the field in battle, or indeed doing anything very much, in case of becoming a breakage. Charles did have periods of lucidity but these were to become fewer and shorter as time went on. While government theoretically remained in the king's hands, the real power was exercised by his uncle, Phillip duke of Burgundy, when the king was mad, and by his brother, Louis duke of Orleans, when he was sane. The two did not get on. Burgundy, who also ruled Flanders, was prepared to come to terms with the English in order to pursue his own interests in France and to protect Flemish trade, whereas Orleans coveted Aquitaine and also had ambitions in Italy (his wife was Italian). Burgundy supported the Pope in Rome (as did England and most Flemings) while Orleans supported the Avignon claimant.

Although Henry IV sent emissaries to the French court assuring them that he stood by Richard's truce (an action that did not find favour with the war party in England) Charles VI and Orleans refused to recognise him as king. And then in 1400 trouble flared once more in Wales. A land dispute involving a Welsh squire, Owain Glyn Dŵr, and an Anglo Welsh marcher lord, Sir Richard Grey of Ruthin, a great friend of Henry IV and a member of his council, had not been resolved to Glyn Dŵr's satisfaction. Glyn Dŵr's family was of impeccably Welsh origins, being descended from a variety of tribal chiefs, but had regularly married into English or Anglo Welsh families – Glyn Dŵr's own wife was a Hanmer, from a family that is still to this day influential in the Welsh marches. Owain had studied law at Westminster and may have accompanied English armies on at least one punitive expedition to Scotland. The failure of Parliament to support Glyn Dŵr was the catalyst for the most serious uprising in Wales since the conquest by Edward I in 1283. It was the result of long-held simmering resentment of the harsh taxation policies of both the Marcher Lords and the central government, the preference given to English settlers and the Anglo Welsh, the lack of career opportunities for local churchmen and administrators, and the unhappiness of local civil servants who had to implement policies with which they did not agree. The rebels invaded the border towns, began the usual burning and looting, and occupied those English castles that had been only lightly garrisoned.

Despite having Richard's body displayed in public to show that he really was dead, there were those who believed, or purported to believe, that the ex-king was still alive, and who were prepared to foment trouble in his name or use the possibility that he was still alive as justification for insurrection. Henry faced a number of rebellions or potential rebellions during his reign, but the most serious was that of the Percy family in 1403. Henry Percy, earl of Northumberland, had been Henry Bolingbroke's ally in the deposition of Richard II and with his son 'Hotspur' was responsible for guarding the northern marches against the Scots.

It was after border raids by both English and Scots that the Percy allegiance began to waver. There had already been arguments as to the cost of policing the marches and how much was paid or not paid to the Percys, and it was said that Henry Percy the younger, Hotspur, had not been reimbursed for his campaigns against the rebels in Wales. Now there was a major dispute as to who should receive the ransom of the Scottish prisoners. In the spring of the following year the impetuous Hotspur was moving south, ostensibly to join the king in another campaign against the Welsh rebels, when he reached Chester on 9 July and proclaimed that Richard II was alive and that Henry IV was a usurper. As Hotspur knew perfectly well that Richard was dead, he could not keep up the pretence that he was alive for long, and as the ranks of the rebel army were being swelled by adherents coming in from the areas around Chester, Hotspur announced that he had discovered that King Richard was in fact dead, murdered by Henry of Lancaster,

AGINCOURT

and that the rightful heir was Edmund Mortimer, earl of March, aged nine. At some stage Hotspur had put out feelers to Owain Glyn Dŵr, and should he be able to join forces with the Welsh – for whom the French had already announced support – then Henry IV's position would be precarious indeed. At this stage the sixteen-year-old Henry of Monmouth, the Prince of Wales and the future King Henry V, was in Shrewsbury as the commander, in name at least, of operations against the Welsh rebels. He and Hotspur had been friends, had campaigned together in Wales and the prince had learned a great deal from the scion of the Percys. Also on the prince's staff in Shrewsbury was Hotspur's uncle, Sir Thomas Percy, earl of Worcester, who on hearing the news promptly took off to join the rebels. If Hotspur's army was to link up with Glyn Dŵr they had to get across the River Severn and they headed for Shrewsbury, intending to cross using the two bridges there.

The king marched on Shrewsbury. On 20 July by a forced march of thirty-two miles – a considerable feat even for a largely mounted army – he reached Shrewsbury just before Hotspur's rebels, who were now faced with only two options: stand and fight, or give up the struggle. Three miles north of Shrewsbury at Hallescote is a low ridge running east to west and about 800 yards long, and it was on that ridge that Hotspur decided to make his stand. He probably mustered around 5,000 troops, the King slightly more. On Sunday morning, 21 July 1403, the royal army marched out from Shrewsbury and formed up on the flat plain south of the ridge, and probably around four or five hundred yards from it. It is not entirely clear how the king deployed his troops. The ground in 1403 it was mostly planted with peas, which grew on canes put into the ground and which thus hindered movement and made it difficult to see much farther than about twenty yards.

Now began a long process of negotiation intended to resolve the dispute without a battle. For most of the day Thomas Westbury, abbot of Shrewsbury, with a royal clerk, scampered back and forth bringing offer and counter offer. The king offered pardon if the rebels submitted, while Hotspur proposed all sorts of constitutional changes that could not possibly be accepted by the king. It is difficult to see how either side could have compromised, and late in the afternoon the king came to the conclusion that Hotspur was deliberately prolonging negotiations in the hope of buying time for reinforcements from Wales to arrive. In fact, although Hotspur did not know it, Owain Glyn Dŵr was at that time a hundred miles away, consulting a fortune teller at Carmarthen, and in any case the Welsh valleys were flooded and would have made any reinforcement from that direction very difficult. The battle could not be avoided and it was opened by the rebel archers. This was the first time that two English armies using the same tactical doctrine had faced each other and at first it seemed that the rebel missile weapon would overcome that of the king. The rebels were on the high ground and could see their target; the royal army had tramped through the peas to get within range and found it difficult to identify what they were shooting at. A contemporary account says that under the rain of rebel arrows the king's soldiers were like 'leaves that fall in the cold weather after frost' and that when the royal archers replied '...on both sides men fell in great numbers, just as the apples fall in autumn when shaken by the south wind'. It seems that at this point a portion of the royal army broke, presumably the rear rank of infantry, fearing that the king had been killed by an arrow. This was partially compensated for by the desertion to the king of a contingent of the rebel army led by its commander one Richard Ramkyn, but the actual process cannot have been as tidy as the simple statement appears. Men moving down the hill towards the royal army would have been assumed to be attackers, not deserters, and as the royal ranks apparently opened to receive them we may suspect that at some stage during the pre-battle negotiations Ramkyn let the royalists know of his intention to change sides .

For all his impetuous nature, Henry Percy was an experienced soldier and must have known that the best plan in his situation would have been to stay on the defensive and let the royal army attack him. This is how the English had been winning battles for the past sixty years and given that Hotspur held the high ground and that he commanded the best archers in England, that would surely have been a winning ploy. That the rebel army now advanced downhill towards the king may not have been Hotspur's intention but forced upon him. Most of the chroniclers agree that in the front rank of the rebel army was a contingent of Scottish knights, commanded by the now visually impaired Archibald earl Douglas. These men, had all been captured at Homildon Hill in 1402, including Douglas who had lost an eye) and had agreed to fight for Hotspur in return for their release free of ransom. The sight of the king's banner, with the king himself clad in plate armour covered in a richly embellished jupon, may have so inflamed Douglas that he cast common sense to the winds and rushed off followed by his Scots, and Hotspur may have felt that he had no option but to support. In any event the rebel infantry, led by Douglas, tramped down the hill and despite suffering casualties from the royal archers, fell upon the king's battle. The royal standard bearer was cut down and fighting was fierce. King Henry had apparently three or possibly four knights wearing identical armour and royal accoutrements to act as decoys, and at least two of them were killed. The fate of England hung in the balance.

It was the young Prince of Wales who saved the day for his father. The chroniclers are as usual infuriatingly vague as to the details of the battle but what seems to have happened is that the rebels crowded towards the king – after all if they could kill or capture him then the battle was over and victory was theirs – with a much lesser press of Hotspur's men facing the left of the royal army. Some accounts say that the Prince of Wales advanced his battle, broke through the rebel line, turned his battle about and attacked the rebels from the rear. This may be crediting the Prince with a higher degree of command and control and ability to manoeuvre than was possible in a chaotic situation where commands passed on by drum, trumpet and banner signals would be difficult to hear and even more difficult to obey, and it seems more likely, that the Prince swung his division round ninety degrees to his right and attacked the rebels in flank. However he achieved it, the prince showed great personal bravery – at some stage, presumably when the armies were at a distance from one another, he had been hit in the face by an arrow but refused to leave the field – and considerable tactical acumen. The advantage had now swung to the royalists and attacked on two sides and outnumbered the rebel army began to disintegrate. When Hotspur was killed in the fighting it was all over bar the slaughter, with those able to extricate themselves trying to get to the horse lines and safety, and those who stood their ground soon in smaller and smaller groups with no course open save surrender or death.

The victory was to King Henry, and mopping up and the pursuit of the fleeing rebels went on until midnight, when the exhausted victors licked their wounds, cleaned their weapons and found somewhere to sleep. The shaft of the arrow that had hit the Prince of Wales had been broken off but the head was still lodged in his upper jaw, and the king's surgeon, John Bradmore, was summoned to extract it. He already had, or had a farrier make, a tool to extract it, first enlarging the wound by pushing a series of wooden dowels coated in honey (which has antiseptic properties) into it. Once the hole was large enough Bradmore inserted his extractor into the socket of the arrowhead, screwed it up so that it gripped, and removed it. In an age without anaesthetics it must have been a long and incredibly painful process, but with a poultice of barley and honey all infection had gone within three weeks. We do not know the exact numbers of dead and wounded on both sides, but it was considerable, and would perhaps have been even more had the royal army had to attack the rebels in their hilltop defensive position. Archibald Douglas was captured, yet again, and having lost an eye at Homildon Hill he lost a testicle this time, and also in the considerable bag was Sir Thomas Percy, earl of Worcester. With the rebel army defeated the reckoning was severe. Thomas Percy could expect no mercy: he had been a trusted adviser to the Prince of Wales and had deserted him. He was beheaded in Shrewsbury the day after the battle, along with the Shropshire knights Sir Richard Vernon and Sir Richard Venables. Hotspur's body was initially buried, and then disinterred and quartered, with Chester, Bristol, Newcastle and London each receiving one quarter, while his head went to be exhibited in York. Other rebels were dealt with summarily or after hasty trials, and in York the head of the Percy family, Henry earl of Northumberland, submitted to the king and asked forgiveness,

AGINCOURT

blaming the whole sorry business on his son, now conveniently dead. While Henry could perfectly reasonably have had the earl executed there and then, he decided to send him before parliament, which body decided that the earl's behaviour fell just short of treason. The old survivor got away with a large fine and the redistribution of his castles and lands to more loyal subjects. There were numerous families that had a soldier on each side of the conflict – there were Calveleys, de Burghs, Masseys, Stanleys, Browes, de Cokes and Greys on both sides and as the most important thing for any medieval noble family was to retain its land, and as being on the wrong side in a civil war meant losing that land, it made sense to back both runners in a two horse race.

Although the king's victory at Shrewsbury put an end to the most serious rebellion of his reign it was not the end of his troubles. The Welsh war was dragging on and Richard II imposters sprang up in all sorts of likely and unlikely places. Money was short and the Parliament of 1404 insisted that the king had quite enough revenue of his own without further taxation, and suggested that he might like to reduce the many grants and pensions that he had awarded since his assumption of the throne. There was no money to pay for supplies for the army and the king's purveyors had to resort to requisition, and when there was no money to pay the troops the officers were told to carry on at their own expense. Despite the lack of money and a hostile parliament, the king survived. He had learned from the example of Richard II who had defied Parliament and the magnates and had paid the price: Henry swallowed his pride and compromised. A small crumb of comfort was gratefully received in 1405 when the French captured the English town of Marck, three miles east of Calais. One of the officers of the Calais garrison, Sir Richard Aston, decided that enough was enough and took a detachment of five hundred men at arms supported by 200 archers, to win it back. An interesting sidelight on the system of ammunition resupply was that with them they took twelve carts of arrows, which must have been more than sufficient as the result was a very pleasing slaughter, with fifteen French knights killed and several hundred prisoners. The commander, the Count of St Pol, a notorious raider of southern English sea ports, fled, divesting himself of his armour as he ran to find his horse. French raids on the Isle of Wight and Dartmouth were robustly driven off, but the fact that they happened at all did nothing to portray the king as a staunch defender of the realm, however hard he tried.

Despite keeping his head and many of his estates in 1403, Henry Percy the elder, earl of Northumberland, had clearly not learned his lesson for in 1405 he was once more involved in rebellion. This time he entered into what was termed the 'Tripartite Indenture', an agreement between himself, Sir Edmund Mortimer, father of the Mortimer claimant to the throne, and Owain Glyn Dŵr, whereby they would depose Henry IV and divide England and Wales between them, with Glyn Dŵr taking Wales and the Marches, Northumberland the north and Mortimer the rest. Whether any of them seriously thought this would actually work, or whether it was just weasel wording to try to cement the alliance can be debated, but in any event the rising was never going to be successful, if only because there was no central coordination and little idea of what to do once armies of sorts had been assembled. One of the principal supporters of the rising was the fifty-five-year-old Archbishop of York, Richard Scrope. Scrope had been promoted to the See of York by Richard II and owed his position more to his father's success as a soldier and loyal servant of the monarchy rather than to any great theological acumen, although being reckoned to be skilled in canon law he had led the deputation that accepted Richard II's supposed voluntary abdication of the throne. He supported Henry IV's accession and was one of the prelates who led him to the throne at his coronation. The rebels' manifesto repeated the usual gripes about oppressive rule and unjust taxation but also maintained that Henry had broken his oath not to depose Richard II.

The rebellion was swiftly eliminated when Ralph Neville, earl of Westmorland, loyalist and a long-term enemy of the Percys, and the kings youngest son, John of Lancaster, marched against them and defeated Archbishop Scrope's hastily assembled and ill armed troops, mainly citizens of York, arresting him and the nineteen year old Sir Thomas Mowbray, earl of Norfolk and earl marshal of England. Northumberland abandoned his erstwhile allies and

AGINCOURT

fled to Scotland. The king intended to show no mercy: rather than hand Scrope over to papal authority, as he had done before to find treasonous bishops given a mere slap on the wrist, he decided that he would go on trial with the other captured nobles. The order went to London to send a team of justices to conduct the trial, and when the country's other senior cleric, Thomas Arundel, Archbishop of Canterbury and a close personal friend of the king, heard that his fellow prelate was to be put on trial before a secular court he rode all day and all night to Bishopthorpe in north Yorkshire, where the king was, no mean feat for a fifty-one year old at the time. Arundel got to Bishopthorpe on 7 June 1405 and pleaded with the king not to execute Scrope, reminding him of the last time a king Henry had been responsible for the killing of an archbishop (Henry II and Becket). The king fobbed his old friend off, sent him to bed, put Scrope on trial that night and had him beheaded with two others the next day. It was the first judicial execution of an archbishop and it caused horror throughout England and Europe. Even if the death sentence was justified (which it surely was) to kill an ordained cleric, never mind an archbishop, was seen as shocking, and allowed Henry's enemies to claim that he had not only murdered an anointed king, but God's chosen servant as well. The pope was said to be appalled and to have laid curses on all involved, but his opposition was short lived and mollified by a monetary payment, while an outbreak of miracle working at Scrope's tomb in York Cathedral did not last much longer. Eventually, in 1408, Pope Gregory XII officially exonerated Henry in return for a promise to found three religious houses. Shortly after the execution Henry fell ill with what some alleged was leprosy. We know now that he did not suffer from that disease to which there was then no cure, but it suited his opponents to put it about that he was being visited by divine punishment for his treatment of Scrope. Whatever it was that ailed the king his health became progressively worse from 1408 onwards and eventually necessitated government being carried on by a council headed by Henry Prince of Wales, which in itself led to disagreements between father and son and led king Henry to suspect his eldest son of plotting rebellion against him.

Meanwhile in France the descent into civil war had prevented effective action to capitalise on Henry of England's problems. Had France been united then, given Henry's financial problems, the French might easily have taken Aquitaine, but with the ever more frequent outbreaks of Charles VI's insanity power was increasingly being garnered by the dukes of Burgundy and Orleans who had very different agendas. Their enmity came to a very public head when on the night of 23 November 1407, only a few days after a supposed reconciliation between the two, the duke of Orleans was set upon in the Paris street and bludgeoned to death, his hand being first cut off to prevent it casting spells on the attackers. The assassination was widely believed to have been at the instigation of the Duke of Burgundy, and he is said to have admitted it some days later. France now split into two armed camps. The cause of the late duke of Orleans was taken up by his son's father-in-law, the Count of Armagnac, who gave his name to the Orleanist faction, and who in broad terms controlled most of France south of the River Loire, less of course English Aquitaine, while the Burgundians held the north – including, crucially, Paris – Flanders and most of the Low countries. Brittany was generally neutral and Normandy too, with divided loyalties, managed to avoid taking sides. The duke of Burgundy had already signed a trade agreement with Henry IV, and as the threat to Calais from Flanders was now lessened, the English wool trade picked up and the English treasury began to look a little healthier.

Then, on 20 March 1413 Henry IV of England died, aged forty-seven. His tomb in Canterbury Cathedral is opposite that of the Black Prince, whose son Henry had put to death, a touch of irony presumably not intended at the time. It is almost as if Henry was two different people: vigorous, an accomplished jouster, well educated, articulate and sociable as Henry Bolingbroke and supported by the vast majority of those who mattered in his unseating of Richard II. Once king, however, he faced uncooperative parliaments and at least eight rebellions during his fourteen-year reign. Increasingly suspicious and dogged by ill health, he survived by compromise, and thus allowed much royal prerogative to be subsumed by Parliament, powers that Parliament would be reluctant to give back. Although Henry maintained the English claim to the French throne – which Richard would have given up – he did little to advance it, and the war during his reign was one of raids, piracy and blockade. Militarily Henry's main preoccupation was the Welsh rising of Owain Glyn Dŵr, and with that and the need to quell rebellion elsewhere there was no money for major expeditions to Europe. Henry did little to change the organisation and tactical deployment of English armies – there was no need – but he did promote the development of cannon, which while present in most armies since the middle of the fourteenth century had little effect so far on the outcome of a battle.

Although the Welsh troubles rumbled on until after Henry's death, above all other factors was that of finance. As the English exchequer grew healthier, English soldiers could be paid and supplies purchased, while Glyn Dŵr had to rely on ransom money and when that ran out to looting his own countrymen – not a policy guaranteed to maintain support for his cause. That the rebellion lasted as long as it did was due to the very sensible Welsh policy of not being drawn into a conventional battle, but to harry, ambush, snipe and raid and then fade away into the hills. But guerrillas cannot win a war all by themselves, and in the end a dogged English policy of attrition, control of the coastline, defence of the Marches and the money to keep going was bound to win in the end, and that it did was very much to the credit of Henry IV. Scotland too was not to be a problem once Northumberland's last foray from there was defeated. It was good intelligence and skilled seamanship in March 1406 that allowed the English navy to capture the heir to the throne of Scotland, James Stewart (later James I of Scotland), off Flamborough Head on his way to school in France, and good luck that his father Robert III died a month later, allowing the English to install yet another king of Scotland in the Tower. James was well treated but remained a prisoner for eighteen years, thus ensuring that England's back door was reasonably secure.

Henry IV may not have been able to pursue the French war, but his son and successor certainly would. By the time he came to the throne Henry of Monmouth had already proved himself as a soldier, at Shrewsbury where he may have been following the guidance of more experienced commanders but where he nevertheless showed great courage and understanding of battle management, and subsequently in the Welsh wars where as his father's health declined the defeat of the insurrection was more and more left to him. He learned how to keep an army in the field in an underdeveloped country and how to conduct sieges, and he fully understood the importance of mobility and sound logistics, all of which would stand him in good stead for his future campaigning. He is generally considered to have been rather fond of wine, women, song and dubious companions during his youth, and he certainly fell out with his father on numerous occasions, sometimes over foreign policy, more often when his father was concerned that young Henry was building an alternative court, but by the time his father died he seems to have put misbehaviour behind him and all chroniclers mention his religious piety.

It is not easy for those of us in the secular, cynical, sceptical twenty-first century to fully comprehend the influence of religion on our medieval ancestors. Religion was, of course, a powerful instrument of social control and an instruction from the king was persuasive; that it was also an instruction from God made it doubly so. Henry V frequently insisted that God was on his side (as indeed he would have been). There were of course men who engaged in what we would today call the scientific method; nobody with any education thought the world was flat; witchcraft and sorcery were largely tolerated until well into the sixteenth century and the Inquisition, which equated witchcraft with heresy and burnt practitioners at the stake, was never allowed into England – as much because it was foreign as for any theological reason. Whether the great men of the realm really believed in the religion of the time is impossible to ascertain but the common man genuinely believed that when he died he would either go to heaven, provided that he had prayed hard enough and had obeyed the dictums of the church, or otherwise would go to a very unpleasant eternity in hell, something that he was continually reminded of every time he glanced at the tympani above the churches' doors. There is no doubting the power and influence of the medieval church. Although it no longer had a monopoly of education – and there was an increasing demand for men who could read, write and do sums for the civil service of an increasingly complex government administration – the church had a finger in most royal and state pies. Archbishops were chancellors, bishops could lead armies, local government in the shires often went with religious appointments and the church was one of the great landowners of the realm as well as being fabulously wealthy. Bishops were members of great families and would have had standing and influence in the church or out of it; much international diplomacy was carried out by clerics while the pope, whether Avignon or Rome, had huge transnational influence. It was, of course, in the interests of the church to maintain the status quo, and in the interests of the secular power – the king – to have the support of the spiritual arm, hence the fear of heresy and the enthusiasm shown in its suppression.

Heresy might be defined as a belief that was in opposition to the orthodox teachings of the church, and anything that struck at the church's power and influence had to be stamped on hard. Up to this point heresy was not a civil crime but a clerical one, to be tried in clerical courts which could impose fines but not the death penalty nor imprisonment. In 1401, however, Archbishop Arundel persuaded the recently crowned Henry IV to make heresy a secular crime, which meant that a man found guilty by a clerical court could be handed over to the civil power and executed – by the rather unpleasant method of burning. Only two heretics were actually burned during Henry IV's reign – it was only obdurate heresy that got a person burned – recantation brought a pardon, and many accused did recant at the last moment, sensible fellows that they were.

Henry of Monmouth, whether a true believer or no, was described as being tall, slim and well-muscled, with hazel eyes and thick brown hair; in character he was said to be single minded – and if he was to pursue the English claims in France he would have to be. Unusually for the time he had no mistresses as king, although there is no suggestion that he was anything but sexually normal. Henry V was crowned at Westminster on Passion Sunday 9 April 1413, the day marked by an unseasonal fall of heavy snow, seen by many as an omen, but of what no one was quite sure. Henry's first task was to assure parliament and the magnates that he intended to govern justly and to heal divisions. While he brought some of his own followers into government he retained many of his father's officials, although he did dismiss the Chief Justice of King's Bench, Sir William Gascoigne. In seeking to heal old sores he released the earl of March, the Ricardian candidate for the throne, from house arrest and had Richard II's body exhumed from King's Langley and reburied with much reverence, pomp and ceremony in the tomb that Richard himself had commissioned in Westminster Abbey. Now Henry could devote all his considerable energies to restoring English rights in France.

AGINCOURT

Chapter Three: Once More unto the Breach...

King at twenty-five, slaughterer of the French nobility at twenty-seven, regent and acknowledged heir to the throne of France at thirty-two and dead at thirty-four. If Henry V had lived the history of Europe might be very different. There cannot be many Englishmen, even today, who do not feel a frisson of pride when they think of Henry V: he shaped English history and what he did and who he was still affects Anglo French relations to this day. A king who deliberately fostered a feeling of Englishness, the first to write his letters in English and to prefer conversing in that language rather than in Norman French, a natural and charismatic leader who if he did not invent English nationalism certainly encouraged it and along with it a pride in nation and in race. While he was a master of propaganda and knew how to use the tricks of oratory, his repeated declaration that his chief concern was for the well-being and good governance of his realm and its people was genuinely meant. Of course he was not a paragon of Christian virtue: he could be cruel and inflexible, ruthless, brutal, devious, short tempered, frequently unreasonable and always convinced that he was under the personal protection of God, but nice men do not win wars and withal Henry V must rank as one of our great kings – if not our greatest.

Well before he ever became king Henry was determined to revive the English claims in France and to pursue them. Once he was king embassies were sent to France and French embassies came to England. Initially he asked only for recognition of Aquitaine as English in full sovereignty, but as each request was turned down the demands became stronger: everything agreed by the Treaty of Brétigny in 1360 was added, then the payment of the rest of Jean II's ransom, then the Duchy of Normandy, until by March 1415, in the requirements placed before the dauphin, Henry was stipulating the return of all the French lands lost by King John two hundred years before, the hand of one of Charles VI's daughters in marriage and the revival of the English claim to the French throne. Throughout Henry emphasised that he only wanted what was his by right, but no French government, of whatever hue, could possible agree to a restoration of the Angevin Empire and although negotiations were allowed to drag on, by the spring of 1414 Henry had realised that the French were merely playing for time and had no intention of even coming to an acceptable compromise, although it is probable that whatever the French might have offered Henry would have wanted more: long before he came to the throne he had determined that he would take an army to France and the negotiations can only have been window dressing.

From early 1414 Henry began to prepare for war. Ships were impressed and purveyors travelled all over the kingdom buying up stores and equipment while captains and individuals were arrayed and indentured. By now the system was that captains and leaders of retinues contracted either with a magnate or direct with the crown to provide a certain number of men of a certain type (archers, men-at-arms, gunners, artisans) at a laid down rate of daily pay, which had not changed in fifty years – 13/4 (£0.67) for a duke, 6/8 (£0.33) for an earl, 4/- (£0.20) for a knight banneret, 2/- (£0.10)for a knight, 1/- (£0.50) for an untitled man-at-arms and 6d (£0.25) for an archer[*]. As the 1/- a day man-at-arms did exactly the same job as a 2/- knight – stand in line with the infantry – there was a powerful incentive to do well and get knighted. For the first six months of a campaign the rule was that the captain was paid half the total sum for his contingent on sealing the indenture, a piece of parchment on which the agreement was written twice and then torn across, with the captain keeping one part and the employer the other. Subsequent disagreements or accusations of forgery could be resolved by matching up the tears. It would then be agreed how subsequent six months periods would be funded. In this campaign indentures were for one year to begin with, which indicates that Henry expected a long war, but in 1414 the crown

---

[*] When this author attended the Royal Military Academy Sandhurst beginning in 1960, the rate of pay for an officer cadet was 10/- (£0.50) per day for the first year, rising to 11/6 (£0.58) (for the second year.

did not have the funds for more than a few months, never mind the initial six months, and even when in November 1414 Parliament granted the king a double subsidy – in effect agreeing that the country would go to war – some of the leaders of retinues and captains were given jewels from the royal treasury as security while the soldiers were paid from the contingent commander's own pocket. Presumably Henry was hoping for an early victory or at least enough loot and ransom money to redeem his jewels and fund the campaign beyond the first six months – a considerable gamble by the ruler of around three million going to war against sixteen million, but then Henry had right, and God, on his side.

Although neither Richard II nor Henry IV had changed the basic structure of English armies, the proportion of archers to men-at-arms had steadily increased since Crecy in 1346. Archers had shown their worth, they were flexible, they could act as light infantry if necessary, being mounted they could act as light cavalry and reconnaissance troops and they were, of course, considerably cheaper than men-at-arms. By now the accepted order of battle was three archers to one man-at-arms, and while not every retinue or contingent was composed of soldiers in that proportion, the king's officials ensured that overall the mix was the right one. Altogether there were around 250 persons who contracted to provide a retinue of troops, varying in size from those of the great magnates such as the dukes of Clarence and Gloucester, brothers of the king, who were to produce 960 and 800 respectively, down to the more humble gentry who might provide ten men or less, and in some cases just the knight and one archer. In addition to the retinues – themselves far more numerous than in any previous English army – there were large numbers of men – mainly archers – who enlisted directly with the crown, rather than joining a retinue. These men would of course have to be formed into sub-units under selected commanders and would have to train together and be instructed in the army's standard operating procedures. The assembly area for the army was laid down as being Southampton, and ships for the voyage were collected there and in other southern English ports, while the retinue commanders held their own musters and then marched to Southampton when ordered.

Originally the king had intended to concentrate the army by 1 July 1415 but inevitably things took longer than hoped. The duke of Gloucester held his muster near Romsey on 16 July and took under command 190 men-at-arms and 610 archers from fifty-six sub retinues, while the duke of Clarence in the New Forest enlisted his 800 from sixty-nine separate units. Altogether there were probably around 12,000 soldiers, of which 9,000 were archers and 3,000 men-at-arms, ready to embark for France, the largest English army ever assembled since the time of Edward III, but the total number would have been much greater than just the combat troops. Henry had also enlisted a company of 120 miners from the Forest of Dean and there were seventy-five artillerymen, numerous bowyers, fletchers, farriers, blacksmiths, armourers, bakers, butchers, and a plethora of servants, grooms, clerks and pages, to say nothing of churchmen and surgeons.

The farriers, whose guild dated from a 1356 charter of Edward III, were particularly important as not only were they responsible for the shoeing of the perhaps 15,000 horses which provided the army with its swift mobility, but they were also the veterinary surgeons. There was normally around one farrier to 600 horses. While there were no paved roads and most of the stone flagged Roman roads were by now overgrown with turf, thus reducing wear on shoes, but heavy going in the waterlogged riverine areas could pull a shoe off, so it is reasonable to suppose that a set of shoes might last for a month. That being so a farrier would have had to shoe twenty horses a day, which while theoretically possible (forty-five minutes to an hour per horse) is unlikely. It is probable that grooms did removes (removing the shoe, trimming the feet and replacing the same shoe) while the farriers were called upon only when new shoes were required. Nevertheless the farriers would have been amongst the most overworked members of the expedition, made worse if they had to contend with an equine disease, such as the outbreak of strangles that hit the Black Prince's expedition in 1356.

The chroniclers generally say that 1,500 ships were needed to transport the force, although some historians consider that to be yet another exaggeration. Altogether the number of men to be

AGINCOURT

embarked may have been in the region of 14,000, not counting the ships' crews, and in addition to horses, baggage carts, stores, rations for men and horses, siege engines, cannon, ammunition for the guns and a resupply of arrows for the archers. Stores included large numbers of tents, and rations included salted meat and fish, flour for bread, ale and beef on the hoof, with their drovers. Given the number of men, horses, cattle and all the accompanying baggage to be transported a huge number of ships would indeed be needed, and given also that both Thomas of Walsingham, generally recognised to be one of the most accurate of contemporary historians, and the anonymous writer of *Gesta Henrici Quinti* who accompanied the expedition, give a figure of 1,500 there seems no reason to doubt it, and wind and weather would preclude any idea of shuttling the force to France using fewer ships.

With such huge numbers of men, animals and ships being concentrated it was impossible to hide that these were warlike preparations, and the French embassies that were still coming and going almost to the last moment were fully aware of what was going on and were reporting it back to their masters. If Henry could not hide that fact that he was assembling an invasion force then he had to conceal its destination. Apart from a very few trusted senior commanders and one or two ships' captains, nobody knew where the invasion force was headed. Most observers and participants, French and English, assumed that the landing would be at Calais, strongly held by the English and on the shortest way across the Channel; others thought the king might repeat the route of Edward III's expedition of 1346 and land somewhere on the Cotentin peninsula in Normandy, or that of the Black Prince in 1356 and launch the invasion from Bordeaux, and it was not until very late in the day that ships crews were informed of their destination, and that only when all troops and stores were on board.

While these warlike preparations were in progress the last serious opposition to the Lancastrian inheritance was snuffed out. When the king was at Porchester, supervising the final arrangements for the expedition, the young earl of March sought an audience and reported the existence of an assassination plot by unreconstructed Ricardians. As the beneficiary of a successful murder would presumably have been the earl, the rightful successor to Richard II by strict primogeniture, this seemingly selfless act was presumably motivated by the earl's realisation that the plotters were incompetent, had no chance of succeeding, and would have been considered to have shown very bad form indeed at the outset of an expedition against the hated enemy, France. The ringleaders of the 'Southampton Plot', including yet another disaffected Scrope, were rounded up and executed after a hasty trial presided over by the king's brother. The embarkation of the men and the loading of stores took three weeks, and on 7 August 1415 King Henry and his immediate staff boarded the *Le Trinite*, the largest ship in the fleet of 500 tons, and hoisted a signal for all ships to concentrate off Southampton. Four days later, on Sunday 11 August 1415 the fleet set sail for France. The destination – Harfleur.

Today there is very little left of medieval Harfleur, and the odd bit of crumbling wall and sluggish stream of the River Lézade that remain are subsumed in the suburbs of the sixteenth century port of Le Havre, but it was a sensible choice for Henry and his army. Situated at the north of the mouth of the River Seine its capture would allow the king the options of striking up the Seine straight for Paris, or west and then south for Rouen and Normandy, as well as giving him a port through which to receive reinforcements. It would also allow him to blockade a major French trading route and – equally important given that the balance of power at sea had tilted towards the French – would eliminate a nest of pirates and prevent French galleys from getting out to sea from the shipyards at Rouen. Good choice it certainly was, and Henry hoped to capture it without too much delay, but in the event it would not be as easy a task as he thought.

The crossing from Southampton took three days and on 14 August the first ships hove to off what the English still called Saint Denis Chef du Caux, since renamed by the French St Andresse, on the coast six and a half miles due west of Harfleur. An amphibious operation, whether of the fifteenth or twenty-first centuries, is at

AGINCOURT

its most vulnerable during the landing, but the French made no attempt to oppose it. They must have known from fishermen that the invasion force was on its way, and had they any sort of coastal watch like that in England they could easily have identified the landing area and caused carnage amongst the disembarking troops struggling up through the surf and the horses and cattle winched over the side to swim to dry land, but as it was Henry's men went unmolested for the three days that it took to get the force ashore. It was at this time that the king issued strict orders as to the behaviour of the troops. The usual practice of slaughtering, burning and looting was to cease: Henry was the legitimate king of France and he was not going to ill-treat his own subjects. No man of the cloth or any woman was to be molested unless they had a weapon and were obviously of aggressive intent, and churches and other sacred places were to be respected. Prostitutes were forbidden to approach the army's encampment and if found in the lines were to have their left arms broken before being expelled. This was presumably a security measure rather than a moral stricture.

On 18 August an advance party under the duke of Clarence marched off to surround Harfleur, just too late to prevent a reinforcement of 400 men-at-arms from slipping in through the south-eastern gate, but in plenty of time to intercept a slow moving convoy of gunpowder and crossbow quarrels from Rouen. Harfleur was around three miles in circumference. It was surrounded by a thick high wall in good repair with a number of towers, and the three gates, on the north-east, south-east and south-west corners were well protected by stout barbicans that had been reinforced by tree trunks driven into the ground and lashed together with packed earth behind. There was a deep stone-lined moat, two spears' length wide (twenty feet) according to one chronicler, to make mining difficult, and a series of banks and ditches on all approaches. The land round about was flat and marshy, and the French soon broached the ditches and flooded much of the countryside. The garrison, now of 700 men-at-arms, was led by a competent commander, the Sire de Goucourt, who had commanded the reinforcements and who had ample guns and sufficient rations to withstand a siege of at least a month, by which time he would surely be relieved from Rouen, only fifty miles or two days forced march away.

Cannon had been of little impact during the campaigns of Edward III and the Black Prince: they may have been used at Crecy and there were some present at the siege of Calais, but they contributed little to the end result. Under Henry IV, however, the science of artillery had progressed, and both defenders and attackers at Harfleur used guns. Eventually guns and gunpowder would force abandonment of the whole medieval defensive and fortification systems, which relied on high walls and moats, and while that time was not yet guns would play an increasingly important part in the war from now on. Henry V had appointed the first Master of Ordnance whose duty it was to supervise the manufacture of cannon and the storage of guns and ammunition in the Tower of London. At this stage most shot was still stone balls, to be replaced by iron later in the war, and cannon barrels were still made of bars of iron held together by hoops of the same material. The powder was unreliable as the type of saltpetre used was slow burning and the practice of 'graining' whereby the right combination of saltpetre, sulphur and charcoal was mixed, liquefied and then dried out to produce a faster burning propellant and hence a higher muzzle velocity, was not yet standard. Guns were still dangerous to their crews and there were some spectacular own goals, when the gunners put in too much powder and only succeeded in bursting the barrel and killing themselves, but if all went well they could discharge projectiles of up to 200 lbs in weight and knock holes in walls (eventually) and they could, if correctly positioned, fire over walls and cause considerable damage to houses and people inside. Guns were still heavy, awkward and of limited range, so while useful in a siege they had yet to fully develop as field artillery.

Having surrounded the town with the army on land and the fleet blockading any approach from the sea, and having stationed men in small requisitioned boats in the rivers that criss-crossed the area, Henry was ready to begin his siege, but as that was the last thing he wanted to do, for it would cost time, men and money, he called upon the garrison to surrender what was, after all, legitimately part of the Duchy of Normandy and therefore Henry's rightful inheritance, with a promise that if they did so they would not be harmed or plundered. Not surprisingly they declined and the siege began. The first problem was to get the English guns close enough to the walls to cause damage, and having decided that the main point of attack would be the eastern wall and the south-eastern gate, the men-at-arms began to dig trenches to allow them to move the guns under cover from enemy crossbowmen and cannon on the town walls. This was a difficult and unpleasant task given the very high water table and the flooding of much of the area, but eventually the guns were able to begin a bombardment against the south-east barbican and the adjacent walls. In order to protect the guns from counter battery fire from the walls, an ingenious system of thick wooden planks reinforced with iron and hinged was devised. Mounted in front of the guns they were raised to allow the guns to fire and then lowered to protect against retaliation. The enemy were not idle. By night they repaired the damage as far as they could, by placing tubs full of earth or sand in any breaches (what would be known as gabions in a later war) and to minimise the effect of stone balls landing inside the town and disintegrating into showers of deadly splinters, the streets were covered in earth and animal dung to absorb the fall of shot. Mindful of the risk of a full scale escalade, de Goucourt ordered barrels of sulphur and quicklime to be placed along the walls, as a blinding agent to be thrown down on attackers, and tubs of oils, pitch and other flammables to be positioned ready to be used against belfries or other siege engines that might try to come up against the walls.

Steadily, and despite the efforts of the defenders to make good the damage, the defences began to crumble and Henry ordered fascines to be prepared. These were bundles of sticks ten feet long and bound together, to be thrown into the moat to allow men to cross and assault the walls, but as this was a highly dangerous business the king decided to try mining first. The Forest of Dean miners were told to dig under the moat and under the walls, and they set to with a will. The problem was that it was impossible to conceal what they were up to from the defenders, even if the ground had not been waterlogged thus making progress painfully slow, and the two attempts at mining were both thwarted by French counter mines. Eventually the duke of Clarence's men captured one of the enemy's ditches and turned it into a strongpoint from which an assault on the walls could be mounted. Then, on 10 September 1415, the army suffered its first major casualty – not from French guns or crossbowmen, but from dysentery. Richard Courtenay, bishop of Norwich, lasted five days and died on Sunday 15 September. Henry sent his body back to England and Courtenay's tomb is behind the high altar in Westminster Abbey. The English had managed to partially flood Harfleur town and that and the broaching of the ditches by the French had allowed sewage to contaminate the water supply. More would die in the days to come until soon it would become a major epidemic. The day after the bishop died the French mounted a sally from the town, and re-captured Clarence's ditch. They were soon driven off but for the rest of the day taunts as to the laziness of the besiegers were shouted from the ramparts. As if in retaliation the next day, 17 September, the barbican fell into English hands and was set on fire in the process. Henry sent heralds to the town to again invite surrender, while ordering the army to prepare to assault the walls. All night the English guns kept up a bombardment on the walls to prevent the defenders from repairing the breaches and to keep them awake, while the men at arms got into position for an attack the following morning.

The attack never happened. In the town damage to houses and to the inhabitants was considerable; the English had diverted the town's water supply, rations were running short and dysentery had made its appearance there too. On the morning of Wednesday 18 September the garrison commander agreed that if he was not relieved by the following Sunday, 22 September, he would give up the town. King Henry accepted hostages from the nobility inside Harfleur; a truce was declared and all shelling, mining and attacks by both sides ceased. As pleas for help had gone out to both the French king and the dauphin, de Goucourt had a reasonable expectation that he would still be rescued; unfortunately for him the king was in the grip of one of his regular bouts of madness and the dauphin was an idle and obese eighteen year old uninterested in the tribulations of his subjects. Not all of Henry's soldiers were happy: if the town was given up by agreement then the possibilities of plunder would be severely limited, whereas a successful assault would, according to the customs of war of the time, permit an unbridled sack and the profits thereof.

On the morning of 22 September 1415 Raul, Sire de Goucourt and the Sire d'Estoutville (commander of the town before the arrival of Goucourt) appeared before King Henry and handed over the keys to the city. The English army began to repair the damage that they had created – the dung barrels by the captured barbican were still smouldering two weeks later – while Henry stated his demands. Those civilians not required to run essential services within Harfleur and soldiers of no monetary value were expelled and escorted out of the army's zone of occupation, while on 27 September de Gaucourt and d'Estouteville and two hundred French knights and men-at-arms were allowed to leave, having promised to report at Calais on 11 November with the cash for their agreed ransoms, or jewels or plate in lieu. King Henry now appointed his uncle Thomas Beaufort, earl of Dorset and Admiral of England, as warden and commander of Harfleur, the garrison to be his own retinue of 100 men-at-arms and 300 archers. By now the health of the army was a serious worry. While battle deaths were not excessive, those from dysentery were mounting, and added to them was an outbreak of what was probably food poisoning from eating unripe fruit, contaminated oysters, undercooked shellfish and prawns, which thrive in sewage. Exact numbers are hard to come by, but according to some estimates around 2,000 English soldiers died and around the same number had to be sent back to England, too ill to continue on campaign. Among these latter were the duke of Clarence, the now totally loyal Edmund Mortimer earl of March, and Thomas Mowbray, second duke of Norfolk and earl marshal of England.

What Henry had hoped would be over in a few days had taken thirty-six, his army had been reduced by a third due to sickness and disease and further by battle casualties and a constant trickle of desertion – always a problem when the army was static and with no immediate battle in sight. Nevertheless, Henry had succeeded in capturing a major port and he had shown himself to be a leader of men and to be concerned about their welfare. All the chroniclers tell how he hardly slept and was constantly around the siege lines at all hours of the day and night encouraging his men – a far cry from the sloth and disinterest of French royalty.

The question was what to do next? It was getting late in the year and given the reduced size of his army going for Paris would be too great a risk, and might in any case persuade the Armagnac and Burgundian factions to unite against him. He could not simply re-embark and return to England – parliament had voted the funds for this expedition and wanted something to show for it, and this early in his reign the young Henry needed a decisive and obvious victory. He wanted to carry out a great chevauchée in the manner of his great-grandfather Edward III or his great uncle the Black Prince, but unlike them he wanted to maintain the fiction that French civilians were his loyal subjects, not to be molested. He would only attack armed bodies, and there were only two possible options: he could head for English Bordeaux, or for English Calais. Bordeaux was 450 miles away overland, a good month's march and by now there would be little forage for the horses and it would be difficult to find food for the men. Calais, on the other hand, was only 170 miles away and Henry calculated that if baggage was cut to a minimum and the army was mounted he could cover that in eight days. There was, of course, just a slight possibility that he might be able to win his great victory without adopting any of the courses open, and he sent a herald off to the dauphin offering to fight him in single combat, the winner to have the crown of France. It was a schoolboyish offer, which the dauphin rightly refused – and given that Henry was fitter, stronger, harder and far more experienced he would have been daft to do otherwise.

AGINCOURT

Chapter Four: Upon Saint Crispin's Day

The army prepared to set out. We can argue about the exact strengths, but it cannot have been more than six thousand – nine hundred men-at-arms and five thousand archers according to the *Gesta* – plus heralds, priests, artisans and servants. They carried rations for eight days, and given that the type of horse ridden by most of the men needs a minimum of 10 lbs of hard feed (oats or barley) and the same weight of hay each day, then a total of around 54 tons of horse fodder would have to be transported, plus spare arrows, tentage, farriers' forges, armourers' kits and food for the men. Some historians have suggested that this entire load was carried on pack animals, but as the best pack horse can only carry a maximum of 250 lbs, then 484 horses would be needed for the fodder of the war horses alone, to say nothing of the feed needed by the pack horses themselves. It seems much more likely that baggage wagons were used, and with horse feed taking up thirty-six standard wagon loads the baggage train, cut to the minimum though it was, would still have been around seventy or eighty wagons and have taken up a mile and a half of road – but a lot easier to handle than herds of pack animals.

Henry's decision to march for Calais rather than sailing away in safety was not universally welcomed. Some in his council pointed out that the French would feel bound to oppose him and that the English would be vastly outnumbered. Henry is reported to have replied that victory in battle was decided not by numbers, but by the will of God, and this phrase was often used in his letters as Prince of Wales during the Welsh wars, when he was writing in Norman French rather than the English which he began to use as king. Whether he really believed that God took a personal interest in the outcome of battles is another matter, but it sounded good and he certainly had great confidence in himself and in his battle-hardened army, depleted though it now was. On Tuesday 8 October reminders as to the prohibition of burning and looting were promulgated and the army marched off in the usual three battles. Two miles north of Harfleur they skirted the fortified village of Montevilliers, still held by the French, who made a sally.

It was a brief scuffle in which a few of Henry's men were killed and three captured. No time was wasted in attempting to take the village and the army moved on. Montevilliers remained in French hands, a constant pinprick to the Harfleur garrison, until 1419 when it was taken as part of the subjugation of upper Normandy. Next day, having covered twenty miles, the army passed Fécamp and again the French garrison made a sally and again they were swiftly seen off, but not before a handful of prisoners were taken on each side. If the intended destination of the English army was not already obvious by their marching north, then intelligence from prisoners would have confirmed the intention to get to Calais. While the French reaction to the invasion had been dilatory in the extreme, it had become clear to the council in Paris and even to the dauphin himself that something must be done, and summonses had been sent out for the French commanders to muster their troops at Rouen, thus being positioned to intercept the English whether they went for Paris, Normandy, Bordeaux or Calais. Now that it was confirmed that the English were marching north for Calais, the French army was ordered to concentrate at Abbeville, with the aim of preventing Henry from crossing the River Somme and forcing him to surrender or starve, or if he did cross to block his route to Calais and force him to give battle, whereupon he and his army would be utterly destroyed, the ridiculous English claim to the French throne would be abandoned for all time and the war would be over. The broad outline of this French plan, if not the detail, would have been known to Henry from prisoners taken, but at this stage he could do little to thwart it – he had to get to Calais.

On 11 October 1415 the English army reached Arques, four miles south-south-east of Dieppe, having covered the very respectable distance of thirty-five miles in twenty-four hours, when they were fired on by guns from the castle in the centre of the town. Heralds galloped up to the castle walls with Henry's message: stop firing and let us pass through the town or we will burn it to the ground. The army passed through Arques without opposition. The following day, another twenty miles nearer Calais, there was a standoff at Eu, where after a brief skirmish a threat to level the town ensured safe passage through it. On 13 October the

AGINCOURT

vanguard of the English army reached Abbeville on the River Somme. Henry had hoped to cross at Blanchetaque, where Edwards III had crossed during his Crecy campaign, but he found all the fords guarded, all the bridges destroyed and a sizeable detachment of the French army waiting on the northern bank. An opposed river crossing was not an option, particularly against a numerically far superior enemy, and so the only course open now was to head south-east along the left (south) bank of the river in the hope of finding a ford or a bridge farther inland where they could cross unopposed. The English army, less burdened by baggage trains and camp followers than were the French, could move faster than their enemy, but not so much faster that they could bounce a crossing easily. On 14 October Henry was south of Amiens, twenty-eight miles from Abbeville, where they were held up on the 15th by the French garrison in the castle of the hamlet of Boves. By now rations were running very short and a bargain was soon struck: Henry would refrain from attacking the castle and burning the hamlet if the garrison and the villagers would provide him with a resupply of bread and wine, although he issued stern strictures to his own men about excess consumption of the latter.

Two days later the English army was at Corbie, only another eight miles upriver, and still they could not shake off the French who continued to shadow them from the opposite bank. Now, however, Henry might be able to steal a march on his enemy. From Amiens inland the valley of the Somme lies roughly west to east, until it gets to Peronne where it executes a sharp right turn and runs north to south. If the English army struck south-east, away from the river, they would have to cover about twenty-five miles before hitting the river again at Nesle, where there was reputed to be a ford, whereas the French would have to march all the way round the bend in the river, a distance of around forty miles, to get to the same place. Nowadays with accurately surveyed maps, air photographs and hand held Global Positioning Systems such a march would be simple, but no such aids existed in the fifteenth century and Henry had to rely on those who had served in the area before, either as routiers or in support of Armagnac or Burgundian factions in France's internal struggles, on local knowledge obtained by questioning civilians and on reports brought in by mounted patrols that ranged far and wide in front of and to the flanks of the army. By this stage a mild form of dysentery, or at least the onset of very loose bowels, had caught up with most of the army and rations had been reduced several times. It was wet and it was cold and there was no time to erect tentage when the army stopped to snatch a few hours rest before continuing their march. Despite all that, by the evening of 18 October the army was within spitting distance of Nesle, and patrols had confirmed that there were two fords, neither more than three feet deep ('no higher than horse's belly') three miles east of the town, and while the approaches were boggy and the French had felled trees across the tracks leading to them, neither was guarded. At the same time the French had only got as far as Peronne, fifteen miles away. That night the English infantry prepared the routes down to the fords and the king issued his orders for the crossing. Knowing that the French army, wherever it was, consisted largely of mounted knights, the archers were ordered to cut stakes, each six feet long and sharpened at both ends that could be driven into the ground as a barrier against cavalry. Although the chronicles say that every archer cut himself a stake, given that the archers would be massed on the wings of the army or on the flanks of the battles, it is more probable that only a proportion of men were to be so equipped – perhaps one in five or one in six.

It was at this stage that it was reported to the king that a pyx had been stolen from a nearby church. A pyx is a box, often made of precious metal, which contains the consecrated wafer that is believed to be the actual body of Christ, and which is used when the priest takes communion to a bedridden or otherwise incapacitated supplicant. To steal such an object was sacrilege and in view of the king's orders that theft of sacred objects would attract the death penalty, unit commanders were ordered to search their men and find the culprit. The thief was found with the pyx, made of copper gilt ('*cupro deaurato*') which he presumably mistook for gold, concealed in his sleeve and was duly hanged outside the church where he had committed the offence. Most modern histories say that the man was an archer, but given the value and importance of this species of soldier, this seems

AGINCOURT

unlikely. Neither Thomas Walsingham nor the *Brut* mention the incident at all, and the *Gesta* simply says that he was an Englishman. It seems more likely that the wretched thief was an expendable asset, and possibly even a servant.

On the morning of 19 October a force of mounted men-at-arms followed by a contingent of archers crossed the fords to no opposition. Dismounting and handing their horses over to horse holders, they formed a bridgehead on the eastern bank to prevent any interference with the crossing. At about 1300 hrs the army began to cross, the baggage and the non-combatants by one ford and the soldiers by the other. One French source claims that the soldiers made a raft from window frames taken from nearby houses, presumably to ferry kit rather than men across. By an hour before last light (around 1630 hrs?) the whole army was across and carrying their stakes and other impedimenta dispersing in the moonlight into billets in nearby villages on the right bank. French cavalry patrols that arrived as the crossing was going on wisely did not interfere, although they would have reported the location of the English army to their superiors.

The French army in the Peronne area was already enormous and growing larger by the day as more contingents trickled in. Many internal quarrels had been temporarily laid aside in the face the larger threat from the English, but large through it was there were major weaknesses, not least in the command structure. As the king, Charles VI, could not be present, being made of glass, and the dauphin was persuaded to stay in Rouen, the Constable, Charles d'Albret, and the Marshal, Jean Boucicault, as the senior military officers of France were nominally in command. While divided command is never a good idea it might have worked were it not for the presence of the king's uncle the duke of Bourbon, the king's brother the duke of Orleans and senior magnates such as the dukes of Alencon and Brittany and the duke of Burgundy's younger brothers, the duke of Brabant and the count of Nevers, along with a host of lesser nobility, none of whom considered themselves to be under the command of anyone and all of whom had to be consulted and pandered to. What all were agreed upon was that the impertinent English must be stamped upon decisively and on 20 October three French heralds appeared demanding that

King Henry state a time and place for a battle. The king replied that he intended to march to Calais, was not hiding in hedgerows and that if the French wanted a battle they could easily find him. The heralds were given a handful of gold coins and sent on their way. On 21 October the English army were past Peronne and traversing the area over which their descendants would fight half a millennium and one year later at the first Battle of the Somme, and crossed the River Ancre, a tributary of the Somme, at Miraumont. The French made no attempt to stop them, presumably because they were now unsure where exactly the English were and in any case were concentrating on finding a blocking position on the road to Calais.

On 22 October the army struggled on, heading west across the valley that would be the scene of the Newfoundland Regiment's disastrous attack on 1 July 1916, through Forceville, Acheux and Beauquesne and then north over the River Authie at Orville and the River Grouche at Lucheux before halting at Bonnières with the vanguard under the duke of York two miles ahead at Frèvent. The duke, Edward of Langley, the son of Edward III's youngest son, was forty-two in 1415 and had a reputation for political intrigue (his brother, Richard earl of Cambridge, was a ringleader of the Southampton Plot earlier in the year and was beheaded for it), but he was a competent and experienced soldier and was on good terms with the king who addressed him as 'cousin'. By now everyone was wet, hungry and exhausted and nearly all had some form of dysentery. Some sources suggest that rather than constantly having to undo and drop and pull up their trousers some men took them off altogether and tied them round their waists. As riding a horse without trousers is an uncomfortable experience this is probably dramatic licence. The rations carried from Harfleur had long been consumed, and that obtained or sequestered on the way had run out, and the men were reduced to eating horseflesh from baggage animals no longer required once their load was exhausted, and nuts scavenged from the woods and hedges. One chronicler bemoans that for the lower ranks there was only water to drink – not as precious as it sounds in an age and a country where most water was contaminated and ale was the healthier refreshment. On 23 October the army was at Blangy, another

AGINCOURT

twelve miles nearer Calais and it was there that they crossed the 'River of Swords' (the Ternoise, another tributary of the Somme), and caught sight of the enemy army.

As the English soldiers struggled across the stream of the Ternoise they saw, drawn up on a ridge a mile in front of them, line after line, battle after battle of mounted knights, armour glinting in the weak sunlight and banners fluttering in such numbers as they had never seen or imagined. Exact numbers are hard to establish: the English chroniclers underestimate the size of the English army and exaggerate that of the French and the French reporters do the reverse, for very obvious reasons. The *Scotichroniconi* puts the size of the French army at 200,000, Thomas of Walsingham says 140,000 and the author of the *Gesta*, who was there, says that the English were outnumbered by thirty to one which would mean around 180,000 Frenchmen. All these estimates are plainly ridiculous, and while apart from the writer of the *Gesta* the English reporters were not there, men who were there and who were spoken to by later chroniclers certainly thought that the French numbers were far greater than they actually were. While clerks and churchmen could be forgiven for being unable to assess numbers accurately, professional soldiers have to be able to make a reasonable estimate of what they might be up against, otherwise they are likely to either refuse battle when they should offer it, or offer it when they should refuse. To this author the most credible theory as to the over estimation by English commanders on 23 October is given by the respected medieval historian Ian Mortimer who points out that in the French army the proportion of men-at-arms to crossbowmen and archers was much greater than it was in the English forces, and that every man-at-arms had at least one page, esquire or a servant, and if these supporters were riding their masters spare horses, then from a distance of a mile or so they would be indistinguishable from combatants. Whatever the true figure it is undeniable that the English were greatly outnumbered: certainly by two to one and perhaps by three to one – not as bad as thirty to one, but a daunting prospect nonetheless.

On seeing the French army forming up in what looked like battle array, King Henry ordered the English army to do likewise, but after an hour or so of staring at each other the French army withdrew, and the English army followed them as far as the hamlet of Maisoncelle, two miles farther on, while patrols reported that the French had taken up a blocking position across the Calais road at Azincourt, a mile to the north-west. It was now obvious to all that there would be a battle the next day. The only way to avoid it would be for King Henry to humble himself and relinquish his claims to the French throne and to English France – which he could not possibly do without forfeiting the loyalty of his subjects, in England and in France. He had already released the prisoners taken along the way from Harfleur, and while this was dressed up as a concession, it was really a way of getting rid of useless mouths who had to be fed and guarded, and that was as far as he was prepared to go. Henry's men had left a trail of vomit and diarrhoea all across northern France; they were starving, sick and wet; their clothes were in rags and they were hugely outnumbered by an enemy operating in its own land. But these were vicious, hard, professional soldiers. They had trounced the Scots, the Welsh, northern rebels and the French time and time again and they had a leader in whom they had absolute confidence, and who had absolute confidence in himself. They would fight on the morrow and they would win, as they always had and if any man thought that they were taking on an impossible task, then he kept that opinion strictly to himself. As Sir David ap Llewellyn of Breconshire was reputed to say, looking at the enemy ranks: 'there are enough to be killed, enough to be taken and enough to run away'. For the men-at-arms the presence of so many French nobles – easily identified by the badges and crests on banners, shields and surcoats – meant increased prospects of riches from ransoms, while for the archers there was a more personal motive. It may not be true that any captured archer had the index and second finger of his right hand cut off to prevent him from drawing a bow again, but archers certainly believed that would be their fate if taken prisoner, and the English V sign of two fingers is said to originate from this period, as archers taunted the enemy ranks by showing that they could still fight.

Shakespeare has King Henry going round his men during the night in disguise, in order to properly assess morale. This is surely nonsense. In a small army which he had personally led since leaving England in August the king would have known perfectly well what state morale was in, and he had enough confidence in his subordinate commanders to know that they would tell him the truth and not what they thought he wanted to hear. Indeed, when sometime during the night Sir Walter Hungerford, a thirty-seven year old who combined military command with diplomatic responsibilities, the speakership of the House of Commons and chancellorship of the Duchy of Lancaster, opined that what they really needed was another ten thousand good English archers, Henry replied that he was perfectly content with what he had and would not accept another man if he was offered him – clearly not true but it sounded good.

In the lines of the French army sprits were high. Unlike their English counterparts who were sleeping in ditches and under bushes there was no shortage of tents and warm comfortable billets in the farms and houses roundabout. Men threw dice to see who would have the most important prisoners, including the English king himself, and the complete silence from the English lines (in fact on the king's orders) made the commanders at one stage worry that their quarry had somehow slipped away and evaded them. Recce patrols confirmed that the English were still there – the silence was presumed to be because they were terrified as to what would happen to them in the morning.

All night long it rained, and the English army slept, or tried to sleep, in a rough battle formation. In truth there was no risk of their being surprised by a night attack – the French high command was simply not capable of organising it, and in any case would have regarded it as dishonourable – there was far more glory to be gained in daylight when all could see the deeds of valour that would surely be performed. A modern army would stand to – that is form up ready for battle in all respects – at first light, but that was not the way of medieval warfare, where breakfast (meagre in the case of the English) had to be taken, final orders given and some encouraging rhetoric promulgated. At around mid-morning of Friday, 25 October 1415, Saint Crispin's Day, King Henry ordered his army to fall in in its three battles, across a field recently sown with winter wheat. The army was too small to have a battle in reserve, so the three divisions lined up abreast, with the duke of York commanding the right, the king the centre and Thomas Baron Camoys the left. Camoys, married to Henry Hotspur's widow, was perhaps an odd choice as a divisional commander: he was sixty-five years old in 1415, he had little experience of command in the field and his personal retinue was only twenty-four men-at-arms and sixty-nine archers, but he was a member of the king's council, had served on numerous royal commissions and was known as a good organiser and administrator. Sixty-five was of course old for field soldiering, but not as old as often claimed. While male life expectancy in fourteenth century England was around thirty-five years this is a misleading statistic, made so by a very high rate of infant mortality – death in childbirth or when very young. A member of the English aristocracy, if he survived to the age of twenty-one, could, assuming he escaped the plague and was not killed in battle, expect to live until the age of sixty-nine. The king had no intention of getting involved in a battle of manoeuvre and Camoys' main responsibility would be to ensure that his men stood – and that they would surely do.

Assuming that casualties and desertions along the way from Harfleur had been made up by reinforcements from England, then the men-at-arms once lined up, probably in four ranks, would have covered a frontage of 250 yards or so and two and a half thousand archers on each wing, probably in ten ranks, would between them add another 500 yards, thus the whole army, from left to right would have taken up a minimum of 750 yards. Henry now ordered the archers to plant their stakes, which were in two rows (possibly more), driven into the ground at an angle so that the point was at the height of a horses brisket and staggered so that a charging horse getting in between two stakes of the front row would run into one in the second. If the stakes were a yard apart this would indicate a total of 1,000 stakes, implying that one in five archers carried a stake. This formation ensured that a cavalry charge would be funnelled away from the archers and towards the English centre where it would come up against infantry in line and be seen off. The baggage wagons were probably in Maisoncelles, with the horses picketed nearby.

AGINCOURT

The army was now in battle array, and while we do not know what King Henry said to them, it must have been something very similar to those wonderful words put in his mouth by Shakespeare, surely one of the most evocative speeches in the English language:

... From this day to the ending of the world,
For we in it shall be remembered.
We few, we happy few, we band of brothers.
For he today that sheds his blood with me shall be my brother;
Be he ne'er so vile, this day shall gentle his condition;
And gentlemen in England now abed shall think themselves accursed they were not here,
And hold their manhoods cheap, whilst any speaks
That fought with us upon Saint Crispin's Day...

The practicalities of addressing six thousand men spread out over a distance of half a mile without a public address system are considerable, even allowing for the fact that medieval orators were accustomed to addressing and being heard by huge crowds – and nearer to our own day WE Gladstone regularly held crowds of ten thousand or more for several hours. The likelihood is that what Henry said was repeated by officers stationed along the front, as was the practice in British armies of the eighteenth and early nineteenth centuries, or that he simply cantered down the line repeating a few words: 'good luck chaps, do your best' as any modern commander might.

King Henry's plan was the tried and tested English tactic: find a favourable bit of ground and wait for the enemy to attack. When it was clear that the enemy were not going to attack, or not just yet, Henry ordered the banners to advance, that is for the signal to be given for the army to move forward. The decision to move was doubtless influenced by the English flanks being unprotected and thus vulnerable to a French encircling movement, had the French been capable of doing that – in reality unlikely but they could very well have despatched cavalry to work its way round behind the English line. The archers uprooted their stakes and the whole army began to move forward in line, across the muddy open fields. When all three divisions and their flanking archers had covered around half a mile or so they were able to anchor their flanks on two woods: the wood of Tramecourt on the right and that of Azincourt on the left. This move was of course risky, as a more competent enemy might have launched an attack to catch the English on the move. Henry was confident, however, that given the distance from the French line there would be ample time for his army to halt and take up the defensive, although an archer trudging through the mud with his stake over his shoulder and wondering whether his very tatty hat was keeping his bowstring dry, may have felt rather less convinced.

Three hundred yards from the French line the English army halted, picked up their dressing and planted their stakes, watched by the enemy host. The size of the French army was such that there was not room for the usual formation of two battles forward and one back in reserve, and the three formations were one behind the other. They had learned something from previous defeats by the English, and the front battle, of around five thousand men-at-arms was formed up dismounted, with the five thousand men of the second battle behind the first and similarly on its feet, while the men of the third battle at the rear, another five thousand or so remained mounted. Other mounted men were stationed on each wing, perhaps two hundred or so in each detachment. Missile support consisted of mercenary crossbowmen and some archers, most placed on the wings in the English fashion but some spread along the front. The standard French military establishment had two men-at-arms for every crossbowman or archer, which would indicate the presence of seven thousand crossbowmen, far more than were actually present, but as in the event they played no part in the battle we need not detain ourselves overmuch in estimating their numbers. There was a French plan, and it was a perfectly sound plan. The battle would open with an attack by the dismounted French vanguard, which would occupy the attention of the English infantry, when the French heavy cavalry on the wings would circle round and take the archers in flank. Once the archers had been driven off then numbers would tell and the English would be slaughtered, probably without even calling upon the second and third battles, although the mounted third battle might be used to pursue the fleeing remnants of Henry's army. It

AGINCOURT

was a perfectly sound plan but in hindsight it was not the best plan that the French could have come up with. They could afford to wait: Henry could not, and if the French had simply waited on the defensive then Henry would have had to either attack them, to his disadvantage, or starve, and even better had the French placed themselves between the two woods, which they could easily have done, instead of allowing the English to anchor their flanks by doing so.

Henry was well aware that his only hope was to make the French attack him. If he could panic them into a precipitate attack so much the better, and the means to do just that was at hand. The overall commander of the archers was the sixty-year-old Sir Thomas Erpingham. A native of East Anglia he had been a soldier from the age of thirteen when he had accompanied his father to Aquitaine in the service of the Black Prince; he had campaigned with John of Gaunt in Spain and with the future King Henry IV in Lithuania, Prussia and Palestine; he had fought the Scots, the Welsh and the French: a true professional there was little that he did not know about soldiering. He had directed his archers to their positions, supervised the hammering in of stakes, the stringing of bows and the placing of each archer's arrows in the ground in front of him, cantering from one flank to another as he ensured that his men knew what they had to do. Now, at a signal from the king, Sir Thomas trotted out ahead of the English line, and hurled his baton in the air. It was the signal for the archers to unloose hell.

In the first thirty seconds twenty-five thousand arrows fell upon the French. The target area was such that no archer needed to pick a specific target; he just had to ensure that his arrow fell within the beaten zone of the French army. The result was chaos, horror and surprise. Shot at extreme range the heavy war arrows falling out of the sky were far too many to dodge, even if the packed ranks of men-at-arms gave any room for ducking and diving, and the only option, so it seemed to someone on the French side – probably one of the royal dukes – was to order an immediate assault by the leading division, which began to move down the slight slope towards the English line. What should have happened now was for the French crossbowmen and archers to provide missile support until the line closed, and for the cavalry then to attack the archers.

It did not happen. The mounted knights on the flanks, stung by clouds of arrows to which they had no reply bundled the crossbowmen out of the way, or rode over them, and launched a headlong charge against the English flanks. Headlong it may have been to start with but over newly ploughed land on which rain had been falling all night it soon slowed to a procession through the mud, with horses sinking to their fetlocks and soon barely out of a trot. Those riders that did cover the three hundred yards between the armies found their horses blown, and their way barred by a hedge of stakes. In the one and a half minutes that the French heavy cavalry would have taken to reach the English the archers would have discharged 75,000 arrows, not all at the horsemen, but enough to wound and kill men and madden and cripple horses. A trained horse will not normally bolt, whatever the situation, and the medieval bit would stop a charging elephant, but not when it is terrified and in pain from arrows stuck in its rump, breast and neck and with blood streaming from its wounds. Heads thrown in the air, riders sawing ineffectually at their mouths, the horses panicked and charged wherever they could to escape the hail of arrows, and in many cases this meant bursting through their own infantry still plodding down the slope. The infantry, already seriously disorganised and disorientated by the arrow storm, and exhausted by struggling through the mud in their full armour were now even more disrupted, but they did, at last, slipping and sliding, hit the English line. Even if only half the leading French division survived to close with their enemy, they still outnumbered the English men-at-arms by two and a half to one, and at first numbers told and the English began to give ground. The fighting was intense, particularly around the centre of each division where the commanders and their banners were. The duke of York was killed on the right, the king himself stood over the stunned body of his brother, the duke of Gloucester, and sustained a severe blow to the head that dented his helmet in the process, but then the archers changed roles and became light infantry. Over the last fifty yards or so of the French advance the archers had been shooting directly at them, and at that range the narrow bodkin arrowhead would go through plate armour causing yet more death and destruction. One the lines closed, however, they had done their duty and no more

AGINCOURT

might have been expected of them. Unlike the French missile arm, however, these were not mere cowed foreign mercenaries but freeborn Englishmen, and dropping their bows and drawing their long knives the archers stepped out from behind their protective stakes and attacked the French in flank. Normally an armoured knight would have nothing to fear from such a lightly armed opponent, but faced by English men-at-arms in front and the knifemen at flank and rear who stabbed though visors and severed hamstrings from behind, the tide of battle quickly turned. The French in front tried to retreat but could not do so in the press of men from the second battle coming behind them, and soon knights and men-at-arms began to surrender, first in ones and twos and then in whole subunits.

It was at this stage that the baggage train came under attack. When the army moved forward from Maisoncelle in the morning the baggage followed, so that the runners bringing the resupply of arrows had less distance to travel. It is uncertain who actually attacked the wagons – it was probably not the third, mounted battle, many of whose members, seeing how the wind blew, or did not blow, had wisely left for home, and it may have been the local landowner with a levy of his tenants who would have known the paths through the woods enabling them to get behind the English without being seen. Whoever it was, the balance could now swing back in favour of the French. The un-blooded third battle might come back, the large number of surrendered knights, outnumbering their captors in many cases, might decide to un-surrender themselves and there were plenty of weapons lying about the field for them to pick up. The only way to ensure that the hundreds – perhaps thousands – of prisoners could not renege and re-start the battle was to kill them, and that is what Henry ordered. The men-at-arms demurred: not only was this extremely bad form but the prisoners represented very large sums of money in the shape of ransoms. The archers had no such inhibitions, and the butchering of the prisoners began. The attack on the baggage train was beaten off, those French who could do so fled, the third battle made no attempt to return and the Battle of Azincourt was over.

It was a great and stunning victory, ranking with Blenheim, Waterloo and Amiens 1918. The French dead included Eduard, duke of Bar, Antoine duke of Brabant, Jean duke of Alencon, Charles d'Albret the Constable, nine counts, ninety barons, 1,500 knights and several thousand lesser nobility, although how many were killed in battle and how many as prisoners is not known. The dukes of Orleans and Bourbon were taken prisoner as were the counts of Richemont, Vendome and Eu, and the Marshal of France. It was the greatest slaughter ever of the French nobility, from which it never really recovered. Today the killing of the prisoners would be regarded as murder and a war crime, but Henry had little option. Many of the prisoners had surrendered many times and had then slipped away when no one was looking. If they were allowed to re-enter the fray Henry's tiny army could yet be defeated. He did what he had to do, and no one at the time – not even the French – criticised him for it. On the English side casualties were few – although probably more than was admitted to, with only the duke of York, the earl of Suffolk and two newly dubbed knights mentioned in the *Gesta* – and if we assume that a French estimate of 600 English dead and wounded is too high, then the real figure is probably three to four hundred.

There was little time to celebrate, for the army still had to get to Calais. The dead bodies were stripped of anything wearable, for English clothing was falling apart, and left for the local peasants to first plunder and then bury. Four days later, on Tuesday 29 October, the army had covered the forty-five miles to Calais and on 16 November, having received the Harfleur prisoners with their ransoms, Henry and his army sailed for Dover.

AGINCOURT

Chapter Five: The End of a Dream

Azincourt was the high water mark of English military supremacy: a mobile army of professional soldiers that dismounted to fight on foot supported by longbowmen had proved unbeatable, there was an officer class that knew what it was doing; with a popular and successful king there was little incentive for internal strife or rebellion, and there was a parliament that was happy to fund English ambitions. The battle was a great boost to English prestige and it terrified the French who, for the time being at least, would avoid facing the English in open battle, preferring instead to lock themselves up in castles and fortified towns. It was not, however a great strategic, as opposed to tactical, victory. A professional army is necessarily a small army and the huge disparity in population meant that to have any realistic chance of subduing the whole of France Henry would need to find allies.

Henry spent most of 1416 in England while the French attempted unsuccessfully to regain Harfleur. In November 1416 the English Parliament met, and agreed with the king that another expedition would be necessary to force the French to see justice. This time Henry would subdue France piece by piece, beginning with Normandy. The money was voted, taxes imposed, loans raised and in the spring of 1417 recruiting of soldiers and impressment of ships began. Henry was well aware that after Azincourt no French army would face him in open field. If he was to bring Normandy back to its true allegiance he would have to do it by capturing the cities, and that meant large quantities of siege engines and cannon with the requisite ammunition. Cannon balls were still mostly of stone, but a primitive form of incendiary shell had been developed consisting of a hollow iron ball stuffed with tow soaked in pitch. The main army of around 10,000 all ranks, in the rough proportion of three archers to one man-at-arms, embarked at Southampton on 30 July and landed at the mouth of the River Touques, just north of Deauville, on 2 August. Progress was swift and Henry was aided by a resurgence of civil war between the Armagnac and Burgundian factions. From the bridgehead at Touques the English navy ferried men, stores and siege engines along the coast and up the River Orne, and the siege of Caen began in mid August 1417. After blocking all routes in and out of Caen and bombarding the city, the English army assaulted over the walls on 4 September. Then began the usual horror of a civilian population in a town stormed by English soldiers, as the men fired up by the lust of battle, and the adrenalin of the attack, took out the death of their comrades and their own dangers on anyone who happened to be foolish enough to be on the streets.

The fate of Caen was salutary: other towns smaller or less well fortified drew the obvious implication and surrendered before they were invested. By November a wide swathe of territory between Verneuil and Alencon had been taken; in the middle of the month the dukes of Brittany, Anjou and Maine signed a treaty of neutrality with Henry, to last for ten months; Falaise, the well-fortified birth place of the Conqueror, held out but after a three months siege fell on 16 February 1418; by the end of March 1418 Bayeux, Saint Lo, Coutances, Avranches and Pontorson had either surrendered or been captured and Cherbourg, at the end of the Cotentin peninsula, capitulated after a five months siege on 27 September. During all this time the Armagnacs were far too busy with the Burgundians to offer any respite to their embattled and besieged compatriots, while Henry studiously avoided any provocation to the duke of Burgundy and was careful not to appear to be threatening Paris – held by the Armagnacs but coveted by the Burgundians.

In June 1418 Louviers fell, a siege personally supervised by the king himself, and as a cannon ball from the defenders had gone right through the royal tent, the gun crew were duly hanged. The capital of Normandy, Rouen, still held out. It was not only a political objective but an enormously rich town which housed the main French shipyards, and although mastery at sea was now firmly in the hands of the English it was important to keep it so and this meant the capture or destruction of the yards. In late July Henry took Pont de l'Arche, just upstream of Rouen, and established an outpost there with a huge chain stretched across the

AGINCOURT

river. With the English already controlling the mouth of the Seine this meant that Rouen was cut off from any relief by water. The town was the strongest yet tackled by the English: the walls were five miles in circumference, the gates were well fortified by barbicans in good repair and there were towers housing cannon at regular intervals. The garrison was commanded by Guy Le Boutellier, an experienced and determined soldier.

By now the English were expert at siegecraft, even if they would much rather not get tied down in doing it, and the king's army surrounded the city. All routes in and out were cut off and the bombardment began. By the autumn the occupiers of Rouen were reduced to eating horses, and when these were all gone the dogs and the cats, followed by rats, were next. On 31 December a group of French knights appeared on the battlements asking for parley. Henry kept them waiting but on 2 January negotiations were opened and the garrison commander agreed that if no relief force appeared by 19 January then he would surrender the city and accept the English terms – which were surprisingly generous. Although an indemnity of 300,000 crowns (£50,000) was to be paid the garrison could march out to safety, without their weapons and having sworn not to take up arms against the English for one year, and civilians who took an oath of allegiance to Henry would not have their houses or property plundered. No relief force appeared, nor was there any likelihood of one, and so the city of Rouen passed into English hands. Henry spent two months repairing the damage and then continued the subjugation of the rest of Normandy. By the end of the year 1419 the whole of the duchy was once more in English hands.

Then came a stroke of luck for England, and Henry got his ally. On 10 September 1419, at Montereau on the River Yonne, forty miles south east of Paris, the duke of Burgundy arrived to pay homage to the twenty-year-old dauphin. As he knelt the Armagnacs, who had no intention of forgetting or forgiving previous Burgundian enmity, struck and Jean was hacked to pieces, his right hand being cut off first, to stop him raising the devil. It was claimed by the Burgundians that the dauphin had personally given the signal for the attack, and true or not the murder sent shock waves throughout France, with many in Paris and the north blaming the dauphin for all the ills that the war had brought upon them. Jean of Burgundy's heir, Phillip, a mature man of twenty-five, was horrified and immediately made overtures to the only man who could help him to exact revenge – Henry V of England. In December 1419 a formal treaty of alliance between England and Burgundy was signed, whereby Phillip would recognise Henry's claim to the French throne and Henry in turn would not interfere with the Burgundian territories other than as the feudal overlord.

From now on it would be Anglo Burgundian armies that would campaign to conquer Dauphinist France, and a combination of the threat of a now far larger military opposition, general war weariness and disgust at the murder of Phillip's father persuaded the supporters of mad king Charles VI to make peace with Henry. The result was the Treaty of Troyes signed on 20 May 1420, which granted Henry almost all that he and his forefathers had asked for. Charles may not have known what he was signing, but the treaty was ratified by the *Parlement* and Henry was recognised as Charles's heir to the French throne, Queen Isabeau, who had long presided over an alternative court in Burgundian territory, having conveniently declared her son the dauphin the product of an adulterous affair and therefore a bastard. The two kingdoms were not to be amalgamated but ruled separately, albeit by the same man, and Henry was required to conquer that portion of France not already pledged to him – which effectively meant south of the River Loire. In the meantime Henry was declared the regent of France and betrothed to Katherine of Valois, the nineteen-year-old daughter of Charles VI. While this was intended as a dynastic marriage pure and simple, it seems that it developed into a genuine love match, and Katherine would eventually become a much loved queen and queen dowager of England. The marriage took place within a fortnight of the treaty being signed, for Henry had no time to waste, and after a brief consummation the combined armies marched off to besiege Montereau, the scene of Duke Jean's assassination.

AGINCOURT

In September Henry made his ceremonial entrance into Paris to general acclaim: the citizens might not like the English but if the price of peace and stability was turning out to cheer the traditional enemy, then so be it. Henry spent Christmas 1420 in the Louvre and then, leaving a garrison in Paris to guard against any revanchist tendencies, set off for England with Katherine. She was crowned queen of England by the Archbishop of Canterbury in Westminster on 21 February 1421 and then the royal couple set off on a progress throughout England, partly to show the people their new queen and partly to enforce the collection of more taxes to support the war. Monies raised in Normandy and France were not yet sufficient to make the continuance of the struggle self-supporting, and while individuals from great nobles to humble archers had done very well out of the war the English treasury had not. Although there were grumbles Parliament agreed the necessary subsidies.

In June 1421 King Henry returned to France with another 6,000 troops and in October 1421 laid siege to Meaux, eighteen miles east of Paris, hoping that it could be taken before the winter set in. That was not to be and as the weather got wetter and colder dysentery and an outbreak of smallpox hit the army. Even the king fell ill and specialist physicians had to be summoned from England to tend him. He appeared to recover, and the siege went on, the only good news being the announcement of the birth of a healthy son to the king and Queen Katherine at Windsor on 6 December. Henry spent Christmas with Charles VI and his now reconciled queen Isabeau in Paris before re-joining his army in the field until eventually, on 9 March 1422, the garrison of Meaux abandoned the town and withdrew into a well defended locality in the suburbs known as the market, where they held out until 10 May. Henry was so exasperated that he had the garrison commander beheaded and his body exhibited upside down on his own gallows.

The English army marched on, responding to a cry for help from the Burgundian town of Cosne, 112 miles south on the Loire, which was being besieged by the Armagnacs, when quite suddenly Henry found he could not ride. He developed a high fever and was transferred to a litter and taken to his castle at Vincennes. The finest medical brains in England and France could do nothing, and although still completely lucid he knew the end was near. After summoning his council and laying down the way in which he wished his two kingdoms to be governed and his infant son to be brought up, he died on 31 August 1422. The greatest Englishman that ever lived was no more. He was only thirty-four.

On his death bed Henry V nominated his thirty-three-year-old brother John of Lancaster, duke of Bedford, as regent of France and guardian of his eight months old infant son, now Henry VI, and his youngest brother, thirty-two-year-old Humphrey, duke of Gloucester, as regent of England. Despite the loss of Henry V, at first all went well, and when Charles VI of Valois died two months later, it seemed that a smooth succession of Henry VI of England as Henri II of France would be achieved, and the baby was duly proclaimed as such. Bedford was not only a competent soldier he was an excellent administrator too, and he was well aware of the need to win what in a later age would be called the Hearts and Minds campaign. Having purged the French civil service of Orleanist sympathisers it worked loyally for him, and despite the provisions of the treaty of Troyes Normandy was still run as a separate territory. Militarily Bedford was ably assisted by Thomas Montague, fourth earl of Salisbury, and his second-in-command Richard Beauchamp, thirteenth earl of Warwick. Richard Beauchamp had served in most of the Lancastrian wars and between them the pair, both in their early forties, directed operations to recover the rest of France. Under those two were a host of thoroughly competent commanders, by no means all of noble blood but who had earned their rank and position by professional ability in the field. All did well out of the wars, most became immensely rich and many acquired French titles and lands which, by and large, they administered fairly and well.

At the height of English power the whole of Normandy, the valley of the Seine, the Isle de France (Paris and its environs), Picardy, much of Maine and Anjou, Aquitaine, Calais and its surroundings and part of Champagne were under English rule, but however benign that rule was to begin with, and Bedford did his best to keep it so, there were problems. The parliament in England

AGINCOURT

was becoming reluctant to raise the money to fund the war, thus taxes in English France, particularly in Normandy, had to rise. There was a sales tax (VAT) a hearth tax (council tax), the *pattis* (road tolls) and an ever increasing tax on alcohol. On top of the officially levied taxes were the depredations of routiers, highwaymen and gangs of brigands, and the unofficial enterprises of many English garrisons which ran what were effectively protection rackets. Feeling amongst the peasantry, initially thankful for an English victory that would bring peace and stability, began to turn. Nevertheless Bedford intended to mount a major campaign in 1424 to subdue the rest of Maine and Anjou and then push south to Bourges and end the war once and for all.

Bedford now began a methodical reduction of Armagnac towns on the Loire. It was not without setbacks, but by 1428 all had been resolved and a major offensive could begin. By mid August the combined Anglo Burgundian armies under Salisbury had captured forty towns and fortified places en route to and in the area of Orléans, the jewel of the Loire, and on 12 October 1428 they laid siege to that town, the capture of which would give England control of the Loire and would trap the dauphin between Aquitaine to the south west, Burgundy to the east and English France to the north.

Then occurred one of the most extraordinary episodes of an extraordinary age. The adventures of the Maid of Orléans, Jeanne d'Arc, Jehanne La Pucelle, the Witch of Orléans, to give only some of her names, had been largely consigned to myth, legend and French folk memory until 1920, when in the aftermath of the First World War that found France on the winning side but with heart and soul ripped out of her, and desperately seeking something of glory and pride in her distant past, Joan became Saint Joan. Jeanne was probably born in 1412, the fourth child of five, in the village of Domrémy (now Domrémy-La-Pucelle) on the borders of the Holy Roman Empire twenty-five miles south west of Nancy and 153 miles east south east of Paris. Her father was a minor official responsible for the collection of taxes, the maintenance of law and order and the general administration of the surrounding area, and he owned, rather than rented, a fifty acre farm with a substantial stone-built house. The transcript of her answers to questions at her eventual trial would suggest that she had an education of some sort and all those questioned at a subsequent investigation twenty-five years after her death are adamant that she was given a good grounding in the Catholic faith and that she was unusually assiduous in attending church.

Sometime around the age of twelve Jeanne began to hear her voices, which she claimed were from various saints and then from God himself. It is not entirely uncommon for girls going through puberty to experience emotional turmoil, but Jeanne was convinced that she really was the recipient of divine instruction and sometime in 1428 attempted to obtain an interview with the captain of the nearest French garrison, Robert de Baudricourt at Vaucouleurs, ten miles to the north. Eventually she was seen by de Baudricourt who, after a number of meetings, became convinced that she did indeed hear the voice of God and that she could help in expelling the English. Baudricourt gave her an escort and sent her off to see the Dauphin at Chinon, who sent her to Poitiers in March 1429 to be examined by a team of Churchmen, an interrogation that went on for eleven days. By now Jeanne was claiming that God had instructed her to go to Orléans where she would lift the siege. It was around this time that she took to wearing men's clothing, a fact that was subsequently held against her, but which may initially have been a simple ploy to avoid molestation on the road, and later as part of her persona as a soldier.

While one's first reaction today might be to write Jeanne off as a mentally disturbed anorectic teenager, there must have been far more to her than that. Medieval man may have been superstitious but he was not stupid, and to convince a hard-baked cynical soldier like Robert de Baudricourt, the dauphin and a host of suspicious churchmen inherently reluctant to grant the right of audience with the Almighty to anyone but themselves, would have required extraordinary powers of persuasion. In the modern age people who hear voices are locked up in lunatic asylums, so assuming that whatever the voices were they were not those of God, the question arises whether she was mad or whether she invented the voices to

AGINCOURT

lend force to her arguments for a military revival. The conclusion must be either that her affliction was confined to the voices, or that she was inventing them. As to what motivated a country girl at the fringes of what would become France to set out to revive, or ignite, French patriotism we cannot know at this distance, but patriot she surely was.

Meanwhile the English had surrounded Orléans, and within a few days had driven the French away from the Les Tourelles, a towered fort that guarded the southern end of the bridge across the Loire. Then, on 27 October 1428, when Salisbury was observing the town from the towers, a lucky cannon shot from the walls took away half his face. He lived in agony for a week and died on 3 November. Command passed to William de la Pole, earl of Suffolk, another example of social mobility in medieval England. William, like many younger sons, sought a career as a soldier, and went to France with Henry V in 1415. When his father, the second earl, was killed at Harfleur, where he himself was wounded, and his elder brother killed at Azincourt, he became the fourth earl at the age of nineteen. The siege dragged on into winter, and rations were running short for both besieged and besieger when an English supply convoy with a military escort of around 1,500 men commanded by the forty-eight year old Sir John Fastolf arrived and allowed Suffolk to tighten the cordon around Orléans, but that was soon nullified when the duke of Burgundy quarrelled with Bedford over the eventual control of the town, flounced out in a fit of pique and left the siege with his men.

Suffolk was able to control the west side and the south bank but could only patrol around the eastern approaches. On 29 April Jeanne herself arrived at Orléans, probably in a convoy of boats bringing supplies. Jeanne seems to have had no problem convincing the garrison commander, the illegitimate son of the murdered duke of Orléans, that she was the answer to his prayers. Clad in armour and carrying a standard that had been blessed in the church of St Saviour in Blois, on 4 May she accompanied a French sally to occupy the fort of St Loup, two miles east of Orléans on the north bank. There was nobody in the fort, but this could be attributed to God's work, and was a much needed morale boost for the French. On 6 May the French, egged on by Jeanne, came out of the Burgundy gate, crossed the river and attacked the fort of St Jean de Blanc on the south side of the river and the fort des Augustins just south of the bridge. This latter gave them a jumping off line for an attack on Les Tourelles and next day they duly attacked and captured it, when Jeanne was wounded in the shoulder by an arrow (as the voices of various saints had predicted), and she crossed the bridge and entered the town. The next day, Sunday 8 May, the English withdrew and the siege of Orléans was over! The French were convinced, then and now, that it was all due to the Maid.

It was, of course, nothing of the sort. The English withdrew because they had bitten off far more than they could chew, they were running out of rations, the Burgundian contingent had gone, money and reinforcements were slow in coming from England and Bedford needed the army elsewhere. While the potential for leadership may be inborn, the execution of it requires training and practice and it is just not remotely credible that a farmer's daughter, however intelligent, with no involvement or previous experience of war could possibly have acquired the campaign management skills to direct the activities of large bodies of troops. It was not Jeanne d'Arc who drove the English out of France but money, population, defecting allies and political infighting at home. There can be little doubt, however, that Jeanne was an inspiration to the French troops, who had become accustomed to being beaten by smaller but far more professional English armies. The French resurgence would have happened anyway, once the dauphin's supporters stopped fighting amongst themselves and concentrated on raising the funds to prosecute the war – and Valois France, which had not been fought over time and again, was potentially far richer than English France.

Jeanne's next ploy was to suggest to the dauphin that he should be crowned in Rheims, the traditional coronation site of French kings, and by careful avoiding of English armies and garrisons the dauphin was duly crowned as Charles VII by the archbishop of Rheims. This had an enormous propaganda effect and persuaded the duke of Burgundy to sign a truce with the French. When the

AGINCOURT

Armagnac army moved towards Paris, egged on by Jeanne, many towns opened their gates to them and they got as far as St Denis before Bedford drove them back and Charles ordered the army to disperse for the winter. Jeanne was furious and constantly urged the resumption of the war. She managed to persuade some of Alencon's men to accompany her and a few minor towns were taken and then lost again. Jeanne's usefulness to Charles VII had now run its course; she had inspired French armies to great things, she had been the motivating spirit for the march to Rheims and the coronation and French soldiers had got almost to Paris with her name on their lips, but she was becoming an embarrassment; more and more she was excluded from council meetings and her supposedly God given advice ignored, and when in May 1430 Burgundian troops were laying siege to Compiègne, despite the supposed truce, she was captured during a French retreat back into the town from an unsuccessful sortie. It has been suggested that the French commander of the Compiègne garrison deliberately closed the gate in her face and allowed her to be captured.

Jeanne was transferred between various Burgundian prisons – and made several attempts to escape – before the English bought her for 10,000 francs or £1,600 and put her on trial in Rouen, the heart of English Normandy. The English had to destroy Jeanne's reputation and while most Englishmen seemed to believe that she was a witch it was not for that that she was put on trial, but on the far more serious charge of heresy. It was vital that Jeanne be found guilty, for by association could be drawn the inference that Charles VII was a heretic too, and also vital that the churchmen who tried her were French and not English. The first trial, before a French bishop, a French Dominican monk and a number of clerical assessors opened in January 1431and ended on 24 May. Jeanne conducted herself well, was careful not to incriminate Charles VII, refused to relate any conversations they had and when faced with a difficult question fell back on invoking the will of God. She denied all charges but finally signed a disavowal of her voices and agreed to stop wearing men's clothing. To the fury of the English she was sentenced not to death, but to life imprisonment. Four days later, however, the English demanded that the court take note that

Jeanne had relapsed by once more cutting her hair short and wearing men's clothing and on 30 May 1431 she was burned at the stake in the Place du Vieux Marché in Rouen.

With the witch burned and the Valois resurgence only just held, the English had to do something to restore prestige and emphasise Bedford's claim that he was the rightful regent for the rightful king, and in December of the same year, 1431, an English bishop crowned the ten year old Henry VI of England as Henri II of France in Notre Dame Cathedral in Paris. It was not lost on the populace that the crowning was carried out by an Englishman and that it was not in Rheims. There was now a military stalemate and once again both sides turned to negotiation, overseen by representatives of the Pope. In 1435 the interested parties gathered at Arras and the horse trading began. It went on for weeks but neither side would budge, and the only result of significance was that the duke of Burgundy formally withdrew from the Treaty of Troyes and renounced his allegiance to Henry VI and II as king of France. This was seen as a disgraceful act of betrayal by the English – as indeed it was – and from now on Burgundy would either stay neutral or, if he fought at all, would do so on the side of the French. It may be that Burgundy realised that once the magnates of Valois France stopped their internecine quarrelling, a far smaller and less rich England could not hold the vast tracts of France that she laid claim to, but in any case the negotiations were abandoned and campaigning went on. In 1435 the French managed to recapture Harfleur and Dieppe. The loss of Harfleur was particularly serious for it meant that English river traffic to and from Rouen would have to run the blockade of French ships, and the loss of Paris the following year was not only a propaganda blow but added weight to those who believed Jeanne d'Arc's prophesy of five years previously. A far greater blow than the loss of Harfleur, however, was the death of the duke of Bedford on 14 September 1435 in Rouen at the age of only forty-six. He was hugely overworked and could have fallen prey to any of a number of possible diseases. With him went the last realistic hope of securing an English France: a consummate diplomat who was genuinely popular, particularly in Normandy, he understood and

AGINCOURT

respected French culture, was a sound strategist and managed to maintain reasonably civilised relationships with most factions, including those of his enemies.

Even had Bedford lived, the English problem was that their forces were vastly overstretched, trying to hold a frontier of 350 miles with Valois France south of the Loire, and another 170 or so miles along the eastern border of Aquitaine. Without allies and without sufficient funds to pay mercenaries, there were simply not enough English soldiers to provide the frontier garrisons to guard against inroads. Mobile English expeditionary forces seeking out French armies and defeating them was one thing: holding the territory thus taken was a very different matter. Further negotiations in 1439 failed, this time over the position of English settlers in Normandy whom England would not dispossess to restore their lands to the original owners, and in 1441 the last English stronghold in the Isle de France, Pontoise twenty miles north west of Paris, fell. In 1444 a truce was agreed and the marriage of Henry VI and II to the fourteen-year-old Margaret of Anjou, whose aunt was the wife of Charles VII was arranged. As it turned out she was a far stronger character than her husband who would eventually fall prey to the Valois madness inherited from his mother, but even at this stage Henry was much more inclined to peace at (almost) any price than his great father would ever have been.

Henry VI was kind, generous, pious and abstemious. He hated bloodshed of any sort and only very reluctantly agreed to executions, frequently pardoning criminals from murderers to petty thieves. He desperately wanted peace with France and would go to almost any lengths to get it. While all these qualities would have been excellent in a country parson, they were not the qualities of a king, and the infighting that went on in the English court as rival blocs jockeyed for power, and the king's own clumsy attempts to make peace under the Francophile urgings of his wife, inevitably had an impact on the war.

The French military revival came as an unpleasant shock in England. At long last Charles VII had decided to be a king and had rooted out the incompetent and corrupt administrators and replaced them with hard faced accountants who were able to raise the taxes that had hitherto gone uncollected. With much of this money he created a new, professional army. At long last the French were beginning to learn the lessons of defeat by the English: instead of going to war with an army of well bred nobles leading a half trained rabble there would be battalions of paid men-at-arms, archers, crossbowmen and light infantry who would not be disbanded at the end of every campaign but retained as a permanent force. In addition he spent money on developing and greatly enlarging the artillery arm. Now tiny bodies of English professionals would no longer find it so easy to beat far larger French armies and the era of English total military supremacy was coming to an end. English soldiers were still better trained, better led and better equipped, but the margin was steadily decreasing and there were not nearly enough of them.

In 1450 following year Caen fell, followed by Falaise in and finally, on 12 August 1450, Cherbourg surrendered and Normandy, except for the off shore islands, now the Channel Islands, was gone. A relief force commanded by Sir John Fastolf never left England. Now only Aquitaine was left, and in late 1450 the French invaded there. Initially there was resistance. Aquitaine had been English since the 12th Century and most *Guyennois* had no wish to change that, but in the absence of a sizeable English army garrisons began to fall. The following year another French army attacked and on 30 June 1451 Bordeaux fell, and Bayonne followed on 20 August. The new French tactics of cannon and bribery were working, and in England there was dismay and confusion. There the magnates were at odds with each other and with the weak king; the rebellion in Kent led by Jack Cade – a far more serious affair than the so-called peasants revolt of 1381 – had only just been put down, money was short and charge and counter charge as to who was to blame for the French debacle were being flung around, sometimes with violence. There was only one man whose reputation was unsullied and who could restore the situation: John Talbot, earl of Shrewsbury, now an old but still vigorous man of sixty-six, released from French captivity with his

AGINCOURT

ransom paid, and in September 1452 he was ordered to take an army to Aquitaine and restore English rule.

Talbot landed at the mouth of the River Gironde on 17 October 1452 with around 2,500 men and marched on Bordeaux. There the citizens rose in revolt, expelled the French garrison and opened the gates to the English. The rising spread, as much against French oppression and taxes as in loyalty to the old regime, and at first it seemed that the *status quo ante* might be restored. Reinforcements for Talbot arrived and a Gascon contingent was raised. But Charles VII spent the winter concentrating a new army and in the spring of 1453 he launched it into Aquitaine. On 17 July 1453 Talbot marched to the relief of the town of Castillon with around 8,000 men and attacked the French artillery redoubt, a deep ditch with a bank behind it on which were mounted cannon, no longer the old bar and hoop type but barrels cast in bronze, brass and a few even in iron. The recent invention of the powder mill meant that the gunpowder used was far more reliable and allowed a much higher muzzle velocity than that available in the earlier years of the war, and as the guns were sited to produce cross fire the result was a murderous hail of iron and stone at a very short range. Even then the fighting went on for nearly an hour as Talbot's men tried desperately to cross the ditch, climb the bank and get at the cannon, but when a Breton force of around 800 infantry suddenly arrived and attacked Talbots's right flank, the end was only a matter of time. Talbot was an easy target: he was the only mounted man, he was not wearing armour (one of the conditions for his release from captivity) and he had an obvious tabard with his coat of arms. A cannon ball felled his horse, and he was killed by a French infantryman with an axe. Large numbers of English were killed and the pursuit went on as far as St Emilion, thirty miles away. Although nobody knew it at the time, it was the last battle of the Hundred Years War.

There were no more troops to send from an England riven with internal strife, and on 19 October 1453 Bordeaux surrendered. Now there was only Calais, and the great adventure was over.

GORDON CORRIGAN

Epilogue

After Castillon English kings never would sit on the throne of France, and the Angevin Empire would never be recreated. What the war did, however, was turn Anglo-Normans into Englishmen and Bretons, Normans, Gascons, Burgundians, men of Anjou, Toulouse and Blois into Frenchmen. At the beginning of the war England was already a united country under a central government. France was not, being a loose confederation of duchies and provinces owing nominal fealty to the king of France who only directly controlled the Isle de France, or the area round Paris. There was little sense of French identity, rather than loyalty to a duchy or province. The war changed that, with the strengthening of the royal government and the population, with some exceptions, now beginning to consider themselves French before local allegiances. The end of the war did not end enmity between the two regional powers, however. Subsequent English kings mounted expeditions to France but with little to show in the long term. Calais remained English until falling to the French in 1558 and Britain (no longer England with the Acts of Union with Scotland in 1707 and Ireland in 1800) fought revolutionary and Napoleonic France for 22 years between 1793 and 1815. Allies *faux de mieux* in the Crimean war but almost at war due to the 'Fashoda incident' in 1898, the *entente cordiale* of 1904 resolved colonial rivalry in Africa and with the encouragement of King Edward VII, very much a Francophile, Britain became less pro German and less anti French. Allies in the First World War when Britain feared a German dominated Europe, after the French surrender in the Second World War the Royal Navy bombarded the French fleet in Mers El Kebir in 1940 and British troops fought those of Vichy France in Syria and Lebanon in 1941 and in Madagascar in 1942. While both countries are now allies as members of NATO, there are those who aver that had the European Union not been dominated by France the United Kingdom would never have left, and as evidence that the legacy of the Hundred Years War is still with us, a French army officer serving in the Elysee Palace told

AGINCOURT

this author that when president of France from 1959 to 1969 General de Gaulle issued strict instructions that on his perambulations around France he was never to be taken within twenty kilometres of Agincourt.

One might speculate as to what might have happened if Henry V had not died prematurely. In time the French might have accepted him, with his Valois queen, but as the parliament in England had made it very clear that in his capacity as king of France Henry could not exercise any power in England, it is probable that at some time the crown of France would have been given to a younger (or older) son and King Charles III of England would not now be Charles VII of France.

Printed in Great Britain
by Amazon